THE
LEARNING
OF
PHYSICAL
SKILLS

Prentice-Hall Foundations of Physical Education Series

JOHN E. NIXON
Series Editor
Stanford University

THE
LEARNING
OF
PHYSICAL
SKILLS

John D. Lawther
The Pennsylvania State University

PRENTICE-HALL, INC., ENGLEWOOD CLIFFS, NEW JERSEY

PRENTICE-HALL INTERNATIONAL, INC., *London*
PRENTICE-HALL OF AUSTRALIA, PTY. LTD., *Sydney*
PRENTICE-HALL OF CANADA, LTD., *Toronto*
PRENTICE-HALL OF INDIA PRIVATE LTD., *New Delhi*
PRENTICE-HALL OF JAPAN, INC., *Tokyo*

Series Preface

The purpose of the *Foundations of Physical Education* series is to provide a set of textbooks which, by presenting selected generalizations from related fields of knowledge, contribute to a sophisticated understanding of physical education as an academic discipline. These validated generalizations provide a sound basis for educational decision-making by teachers, coaches, supervisors, and administrators at all school levels.

Physical education currently is defined as the art and science of voluntary, purposeful human movement. Its central concern is man engaging in selected motor performances and the meaning and significance of these experiences. Thus, physical education is a broad cross-disciplinary subject. It requires of its scholars and practitioners a command of the most relevant generalizations, being generated in the closely related disciplines, which describe and explain phenomena associated with human movement. Those disciplines which provide the most relevant foundational knowledge for physical education are physiology, neurology, psychology, sociology, anthropology, history, philosophy, anatomy, and kinesiology.

Present physical education texts generally fail to treat in depth relevant generalizations from related disciplines. In these books, one or two physical education authors have attempted to present a series of "principles" of physical education in a few chapters, each of which contains some reference to knowledge in various fields. In today's world of rapidly expanding knowledge, one or two authors can no longer be well versed in several disciplines sufficiently to write principles and foundations books in physical education, which possess the depth and sophistication required to understand and describe the field, and to guide its practices.

With rare exceptions, scholars of other disciplines have not devoted their major attention to investigation and reports which concern physical education phenomena. Thus, for example, the historians have virtually neglected the history of sport in general history books and few sociologists have studied sports as their major line of inquiry.

Nonetheless a vast accumulation of knowledge exists in the literature of the foundation fields which has direct and essential relevance to physical education. Most of this knowledge has not been accumulated systematically or reported and interpreted accurately to the physical education profession. The task of selecting and reporting relevant generalizations from any one discipline requires a physical education scholar who is also a scholar of the related subject.

For the first time in physical education literature, this series incorporates books about physical education, prepared by distinguished physical education scholars, who have established reputations for knowledge and competence in the subject matter and in the principal modes of inquiry in the related fields. Thus, each volume synthesizes recent knowledge into usable form for students and teachers and is unique in physical education literature. Furthermore, the reader is instructed in the process of developing his own *principles* of physical education from his increasing knowledge and understanding. Comprehensive bibliographies list basic references for further study in each field.

This series is appropriate for Foundations or Principles of Physical Education courses at both the undergraduate and graduate levels. Individual volumes are suitable for courses concerning their respective subject areas. Also, these books are valuable for collateral reading and can provide the basis for individual study projects.

The series provides a reference source for the latest knowledge of scientific, behavioral, and humanistic insight and understanding, which constitute the subject and the practice of physical education today. It belongs in the library of every student and teacher of physical education.

J. N.

Preface

A basic purpose of physical education is the acquisition of physical skills. Health and physical fitness are important aspects of physical education but are meaningless unless they help bring about improvement in human function, and human function implies expression. Expression is of necessity physical; and skill in that expression involves the social, recreational, and sport skills, as well as artistic expression in the dance. It also involves the achievement of precision in body-control skills which are advantageous in vocational as well as leisure pursuits.

Some years ago it became apparent that methods courses in physical education were very inadequate without a thorough background in motor learning. A seminar in motor learning was started for graduate students and much of the content of this text grew out of the work in this course. Numerous master and doctoral students at The Pennsylvania State University have contributed through their thesis research. The students in the seminar over the last fifteen years have stimulated constant revisions and supplements to the content covered in the course; graduate students at the University of Colorado and at the University of Oregon also have added their contributions.

Two former students of the writer have read much of the manuscript during the writing, and have made invaluable criticisms. Dr. Pearl Berlin of Wayne University read the first three-fourths of the manuscript and furnished some very stimulating and very constructive suggestions. Dr. Joan Nessler of The Pennsylvania State University contributed much by reading the manuscript and suggesting points which needed clarifying. Dr. Nessler also rechecked the footnotes and references.

The writer is deeply grateful to those authors and publishing firms who have so generously permitted use of quotations from or reference to their publications. He is deeply obligated to his former students for the thinking and discussion which have helped develop this content.

J. D. L.

Contents

Modern Man
and His
Progressive Adaptation

LESSONS FROM MAN'S EXPERIENCE ARE
HANDED DOWN TO SUCCEEDING GENERATIONS

It took man thousands of years to develop the ability to read and write but now every normal primary-age child with educational opportunity can read and write. Actually, some children have learned to read by the age of four. The modern high school graduate has a store of knowledge which surpasses that of the most learned men of ancient times. With regard to physical development, man is today bigger and stronger, and possesses more physical skill than any preceding generation in history. The average college man of today is three to four inches taller and fifteen to twenty pounds heavier than his predecessor of just fifty years ago.

The modern giants of sport far surpass in size the outstanding athletes of the past. From the armor of the knights of the middle ages we learn that the men of historical legend and achievement were little more than five feet tall. Some centers in professional basketball today are seven feet tall or taller, and the centers on the great university basketball teams usually range from six feet, nine inches, to more than seven feet in height. Defensive tackles and ends in professional football are usually well over six feet in height and range in weight from 250 to well over 300 pounds. Moreover, sport records are constantly being established and quickly bettered. The four-minute mile, considered as an impossible achievement in the early part of the twentieth century, is today being surpassed in almost every important track meet. The pole vault record has now passed seventeen feet, and the shot put, seventy feet. Even in archery, in spite of folk tales of Wilhelm Tell, Robin Hood, or the American Indian, modern archers excel all predecessors, in both the development of the equipment and their skill in its use.

Increase in human growth is due to man's application of the heritage of knowledge about health and nutrition, as well as to economic conditions which permit its application to each succeeding generation. The improvement in so many types of physical performance is due to man's ability to communicate and to pass on his experience, vicariously, to succeeding generations. The child can profit from the cumulative, epitomized, abstracted experience of centuries of predecessors. Fortunately man, as contrasted with animals, can learn much of this handed-down knowledge without suffering all the handicaps and failures of the original experiences. Man's "learning by doing" can be arranged by his teachers so that it involves faster, safer, less painful, more efficient methods.

LEARNING IS RELATIVELY PERMANENT CHANGE RESULTING FROM TRAINING AND EXPERIENCE

It is readily observable that the actions of a human being, his ways of thinking and behaving, change with training and experience. He modifies his responses to various situations, often to remarkable degrees, after motivated practice and meaningful experience. Moreover, many of these changes become relatively persistent, either in terms of the nature of response or, what is more likely in the learning of physical skills, in terms of progressive adaptation; *i.e.,* his responses become more and more precise, more and more effective in bringing about desired results, and more and more automatic in adapting to varying conditions.

It is necessary to define learning as change due to training and experience in order to make it distinct from the changes due to either growth or its opposite, deteriorations caused by senescence. Moreover, persistence or relative permanence should be considered a criterion of learning in order to discount temporary changes in performance due to fatigue, change in motivation, or temporary physiological fluctuation.

PHYSIOLOGICAL BASES OF LEARNING: COMPUTER ANALOGY

We know that changes in response occur after meaningful experience or motivated practice but the physiological basis of this learning can still be described only hypothetically. Perhaps the most commonly accepted hypothesis as to the physiological basis for human learning is the belief that the human brain and nervous system are analogous to the electronic computer into which are fed the data flowing in from the various sense organs and sensory nerve endings, and out of which flow the currents to activate the responses computed in terms of the many and varied incoming data. The extremely complex nervous system, from higher cortical areas through peripheral sensory and motor nerve endings, with its innumerable input and outflow mechanisms, defies complete analysis, although we do know something of its system of proprioceptive facilitation with continuous sensory feedback, the cord and midbrain servomechanisms, and the sensory, motor, and large association areas of the brain itself. All are connected through internuncial neurons to outlets of peripherally disposed motor units. Herrick once estimated that "the human cerebral cortex alone contains some 9280 million nerve-cells . . . which stretch away for great distances . . . connecting each cell with many different nerve-centers . . . and that "the total number of possible nervous pathways is, therefore, inconceivably great." [1]

This system, with its extremely complex integrative areas, may develop with experience into a marvelous "electronic computer" which continuously takes in data from the various sensory nerves, reassembles these various data in terms of previous experience already programmed into the computer, and turns out response solutions. The complex of inflowing stimuli sensations is received, analyzed, synthesized; and the computed adjustment is sent on, for action, through the efferent nerves and the associated musculature. Actual overt responses are continually readjusted, at times even after they are initiated, as additional incoming cues arrive, and they are acted upon in terms of the great amount of past experience already programmed into this computer. The individual's accumulating experiences, as life goes on, make possible finer and finer "computations" and response adjustments in terms of this richer experiential background.[2]

SERVOMECHANISMS AND FEEDBACK: READJUSTMENTS DURING RESPONSE

The infant reaching for a button on the floor, a marble, or a piece of lint on the carpet can be seen to be readjusting his movements during the action as his hand approaches the object, with such corrections continuing until his fingers and thumb arrive and take hold of the object. This early adjustment of prehension is a simple example of the servomechanism of the human body with its continual feedback of cues and the subsequent automatic readjustment. Children's games of tag, their hunting and pursuit games, and later, the readjustments in team games of already initiated action, all involve this continual feedback and readjustment of response in terms of additional cues which arrive after the action has begun. The almost automatic readjustment made by the highly skilled skater, after he has made an unintentional slip or error, disguises the error so that it seems to be a planned act in the succeeding routine, which flows from and through the error deviation and makes the whole a continuity and a harmony of movement. Only feedback and automatic loop-control could effect such rapid readjustments of acts already under way. Of course, wide previous experience in such adjustments

---

[1] C. Judson Herrick, *Introduction to Neurology,* 3rd ed., 1922, p. 28.

[2] The cybernetic hypothesis as to the nature of human behavior controls was first proposed by Norbert Wiener. For his latest discussion, consult his *Cybernetics,* 2nd ed. (New York: Massachusetts Institute of Technology Press, and John Wiley & Sons, Inc., 1961). See also K. U. Smith and M. F. Smith, *Cybernetic Principles of Learning and Educational Design* (New York: Holt, Rinehart, & Winston, Inc., 1966).

must be "programmed into the computer" or such readjustments cannot be made.

DEFINITION OF MOTOR LEARNING; LEARNING HIERARCHIES

We have already defined learning as relatively permanent change in behavior resulting from experience, as contrasted with changes due to growth, aging, fatigue, or temporary physiological fluctuations. Now we need to define that particular category of learning called "motor learning." Motor learning is usually defined as learning in which bodily movements play a major part; it is a term used to describe an adjustment of responses to some environmental situation, a considerable part of which adjustment consists of patterned muscular contractions, static and dynamic. The bodily movements involved are patterns of responses to recognized stimuli; *i.e.*, they are perceptual-motor responses.[3] The stimuli may be visual, auditory, kinesthetic, or any other sense stimuli or combinations of several.

LEARNING IS ADAPTATION AND PROGRESSION

The relatively permanent change in behavior resulting from experience and training, called learning, is both a process of adaptation to the environment and a progression from simple adjustments to more and more complex and sophisticated adjustments. Just as sounds develop into meaningful words and words grow with use into wider and more explicit meanings, so the simple balance and movement skills combine into the more complex skills of posture and the innumerable body-control acts. Skills advance in hierarchies of development. As McGeoch says:

> After small amounts of learning early in the life of the individual, every instance of learning is a function of the already existent learned organization of the subject; that is, all learning is influenced by transfer.[4]

Perhaps an example from physical development will clarify McGeoch's point. The child learns to balance himself on two feet and transfers much of this balance skill into his development of walking ability; then he utilizes the additional balance and body control gained from the walking development to accelerate his acquirement of ability to run. Running progresses until it includes ability to make quick changes in direction. Now he can utilize much of this learning to play hunting and chasing games. These various balances

---

[3] The implication here is that the stimuli are received and responded to in terms of past learning. However, the use of the word "perception" may be slightly misleading in this case if the assumption is made that the recognition of stimulus occurs at the level of conscious awareness, for a great many of the detailed adjustments of motor responses occur below this level. This point will be developed more fully later in the text.

[4] John McGeoch, *The Psychology of Human Learning* (New York: Longmans, Green & Co., Inc., 1942), p. 445.

and mobility controls are next built into more complex hierarchies of skills in group play. Note the many static and dynamic postural and movement controls on which he builds his sociomotor skills in dual sports, team contests, or the various dances. This progression is what is meant by "transfer" as used here.

The error in many studies which report lack of transfer from one physical activity to another is that the control groups used in the research already have these long-established bases to build on. The relatively short training of the experimental groups in a specific activity may add little or nothing to another specific skill, but these postural and dynamic body controls are already far advanced in both the experimental and the control groups. Beyond these bases, highly precise pattern transfer must depend on considerable similarity in movement patterns; *e.g.*, transfer from baseball to softball or from tennis to squash.

NATURE OF LEARNING CHANGES
FROM INFANCY TO MATURITY

Hebb says that "the first learning of primates is extremely slow, and very different from that at maturity." He continues:

> There are two kinds of learning. One is that of the newborn infant, or (as it still may occur in exceptional conditions in adults) the visual learning of the adult reared in darkness or with congenital cataract; the other that of the normal adult.[5]

Hebb then calls attention to Senden's account of the extremely slow perceptual learning of a patient who was born blind and was then given sight after motor and speech habits had developed.[6] Later he describes the very slow perceptual learning of Miner's highly intelligent patient who had congenital cataracts but had sight restored at adulthood by an operation. Hebb states: ". . . two years after operation [the patient] had learned to recognize only four or five faces and in daily conferences with two persons for a month did not learn to recognize them by vision."[7] The parallel between these two adult cases and the early primary learning of the human infant is apparent.

One must remember that the human infant works at motor learning very steadily from birth on. The preponderance of this type of slow-increment learning during the first year or two of life must not be overlooked in the analysis of human motor learning.

The simple integration of movements into useful patterns may continually progress. Each succeeding skill is made up of, and built on the base of such

---

[5] D. O. Hebb, *The Organization of Behavior* (New York: Science Editions, Inc., 1961), p. 111.

[6] M. V. Senden, *Raum- und Gestaltauffassung bei operierten Blindgeborenen vor und nach der Operation* (Leipzig: J. A. Barth, 1932); James B. Miner, "A Case of Vision Acquired in Adult Life," *Psychological Review Monograph Supplements,* VI:5 (March 1905), 108–18.

[7] Hebb, *op. cit.,* p. 114.

simple skills as the individual already possesses, providing they can be used appropriately. Although the new skill, the new step in the hierarchy, is made up of simpler, already learned skills, the new unit is more than an aggregate of the old skills. It is a fusion somewhat analogous to that of a chemical compound resulting from the combination of various elements, nonrecognizable in their new form. Each stage of learning is built on the already learned organization; hence the very nature of the learning process changes. As Hebb says:

> It is proposed that the characteristics of learning undergo an important change as the animal grows, particularly in higher mammals; that all learning tends to utilize and build on any earlier learning, and, finally, that the learning of the mature animal owes its efficiency to the slow and inefficient learning that has gone before. . . .[8]

MATURATION AND LEARNING

Let us look more carefully at this infancy development, its slow rate and its nature. The newborn infant develops the ability to raise his head, coordinate his eye movements, raise head and upper trunk together, reach out and grasp things. Posture develops posteriorly until he can sit erect. Soon he begins to crawl and then to walk. The development of these controls is both posterior and outward (gross to small musculature) in direction. For the first fifteen months these developments seem to progress in the same sequence in all infants.

The rate of development of the so-called phylogenetic movements such as grasping, reaching, creeping, or crawling shows little or no acceleration in specially trained children beyond that of nontrained children. However, training is essential for the learning of the ontogenetic types of activities— using eating utensils, buttoning clothes, toilet routines, cutting out pictures, and, at higher levels, swimming and skating. The ontogenetic types of behavior seem to be highly dependent on training and experience for their development. In general, as the skill increases in complexity, the value of special training and experience becomes very evident. Although phylogenetic developments seem to progress at about the same rate in an infant regardless of special practice or of adults' attempts to teach and accelerate, the rate of achievement of the developments varies from infant to infant. These variations, except in extreme degree, have little significance for prognosis of future traits or abilities.

Authorities are not in agreement as to the extent to which learning is involved in the infant's acquiring the ability to make individual movements. Some think that a large part of this early development is due to maturation. The child does begin to move in the womb long before birth, as mothers may well testify. From the moment of birth, most infants move almost constantly when awake, and even a great deal when asleep. Between the time of his first movements in the womb and the time he first begins to walk,

---

[8] *Ibid.*, p. 109.

the infant will have made almost every possible gross movement (in the sense of body or limb responses to his innumerable muscular contractions). As the child grows and matures, his strengths, endurances, lever lengths, speeds, etc., will naturally change. Nevertheless, we must admit, after observing even one normal infant, that the almost ceaseless bodily activity includes most of the muscle contractions, hence movements, which he will use and combine into the skills of his later life.

This multiplicity of more or less random movement is the child's response to internal and external environmental stimuli, and results in changes in the nature of these movements. To the extent that the direction of this change and its limits are predetermined by his genetic constitution, it should perhaps be considered maturation, although in the sense that this change depends on environmental stimuli for its development, it might be looked upon as a kind of physiological learning.

No real distinction between maturation and learning in the infant's development can be made because hereditary factors are only developed in response to environment, and acquired factors can only be secured through a modification of already existing structure. In all maturation there is learning, and in all childhood learning there is hereditary maturation.[9]

The distinction between maturation and learning during infancy is only academic. What we should realize is that most of the basic skills demanded by society (eating skills, toilet skills, conduct with others) are subject to adjustment through environmental experience. The eating skills with the cup or spoon are acquired more rapidly if the child is permitted much practice without forcing and without much censure for failure to achieve adult standards. The mother who gets too upset over the mess the child makes may retard his learning. As he begins to be mobile and branch out in his play, he needs equipment, space, opportunity, and occasional help or encouragement.

INDIVIDUATION: MOVEMENT LEARNING

The degree to which movement development is due to maturation or to learning (and the distinction is a matter of degree, not character), is unimportant to us if we keep in mind that any kind of growth depends on a fostering environment. What we need to know is that new movements may be learned, and/or may be individuated from what was previously a gross-action response. It is important to understand this principle and the learning methods involved because much motor reeducation of the disabled and some superior achievements of highly skilled athletes necessitate special attention to these procedures in learning; *i.e.,* focus on and development of ability to control voluntarily a specific movement previously not subject to voluntary control.

Individuation of body-part movements is a major aspect in much of our motor-skill learning. In learning motor behavior, one has to reduce the gross

---

[9] See Leonard Carmichael, "Heredity and Environment: Are they Antithetical?" *Journal of Abnormal and Social Psychology,* XX:3 (October 1925), 257.

acts to certain sequences of individuation. Individuation means a partial dissociation of the specific movements needed for a specific purpose from the gross total-body acts involving extraneous movements—movements not only unnecessary for the immediate purpose but also disturbing to its precision. Observation of a novice attempting almost any skill will reveal this excess movement and excess large-muscle activity, particularly if the skill is one requiring considerable precision of control. Drawing and handwriting by kindergarten and primary school children are good examples. At first, the child tenses much of his large musculature and gets much of his body into the act.

Novices learning any of our sport skills which require precise wrist, hand, and finger control will reveal difficulties in separating the timing, the force, and the direction of the act from the handicapping effects of gross bodily muscular activity. Individuation to divorce the excess of movement, unnecessary for the immediate purpose, is part of the motor learning. The integration of these partially individuated movements into patterns of response to the playback of perceptual cues develops to some degree during their individuation, so that greater individuation often means progressive adaptation.

LEARNING A NEW MOVEMENT
VS. MOTOR PATTERN LEARNING

In methods of attack, the problems of isolating and controlling specific movements and of learning skills (motor pattern learning) are quite dissimilar. For most efficient practice in skill learning, at least at the earlier stages, the attention is not on the specific movements but on the purpose, object, or goal and, at most, only on a "gross-framework-idea" of an action pattern to attain the goal. When the subject tries to be successful in hitting a target by a throwing act, he learns fastest if he focuses on the target with only a gross-outline-idea of the total throwing act present in the periphery of his attention. However, when he consciously tries to individuate a movement for the purpose of learning to separate out and voluntarily control that movement, he focuses his attention on the specific body part in which he is trying to isolate the contraction. The process is, first, to exercise the muscle through some gross act which includes some action of the specific muscle movement, perhaps only as a synergistic action. This action may serve to strengthen the specific muscle toward which the training is being directed, a procedure often necessary in reeducation work with the disabled. Once the muscle can be made to act with the attention focused on it, one practices to divorce it from the gross act and gradually train it to act as a prime mover.

The yogi of India trains himself in voluntary control of body-part movements, which most of us never learn, nor have any need to learn. A few dancers have developed the ability to move independently certain parts of their bodies which in the average person are not under individuated control. During World War II some of the G.I.'s quartered out on the Pacific Islands for long spells at a time learned to individuate the muscles under their tattoo pictures of the hula girls on their forearms so that the figures seemed to come alive. The easiest example of a new movement individuation for the average person to try to learn is that of wiggling the ears. Most people have never individuated the movements involved in this rather ludicrous act. Not only is the act of little value except for a clown, but it may even have a social stigma attached.

Some of the speech sounds of foreign languages seem to involve muscle movements which the average student has never subjected to individuated voluntary control. Hindustani has some speech distinctions which the untrained ear of the American cannot even detect. The trilled "r" of the French language involves movement individuation unfamiliar to many American children; so do the "rr" in Spanish and the umlaut "o" (ö) in German. Verbal explanation is of little help to the novice in these areas. Highly skilled and complex motor performances, whether they be piano playing, ballet dancing, or new and novel routines in gymnastics, may include an individual movement of some body part over which we have not developed such independent (individuated) control. The recent developments by tumblers and divers of double and triple twists in the air probably include some such learning.

PROCEDURES FOR INDIVIDUATING
BODY-PART MOVEMENTS

There are certain helpful procedures for use in learning to separate out a new movement and control it voluntarily; *i.e.,* for use in learning to move a body part independently which has always moved in conjunction with others (ring finger, for example). If the body part is not subject to voluntary control, we move the associated parts and try to move the new part with them (move jaw and scalp muscles to move ear). We try to focus attention and strong emotionally toned stimuli toward the part we wish to move until we can get some kind of a spill-over of energy into the musculature of that part; thereby we produce the movement and also see, feel, and identify it (the seeing may be with the help of a mirror). Our next problem is to relax so that the tension will leave the associated but extraneous musculature. From here on, one should practice in an attempt to improve.

In her "Electromyographic Demonstration of Facilitation," Partridge clarifies this process of strengthening and individuating a muscle movement.[10] Because of reflex linkage, activity may be produced by impulses arising proprioceptively in other components of the synergy. This is the basic principle involved in the individuation of movement.[11]

The foregoing description of the adult trying to learn to isolate a new movement and to subject it to voluntary control must not be taken as an

---

[10] Miriam J. Partridge, "Electromyographic Demonstration of Facilitation," *Physical Therapy Review,* XXXIV:5 (May 1954), 227–33.

[11] See Ernst Gellhorn, *Physiological Foundations of Neurology and Psychiatry* (Minneapolis: University of Minnesota Press, 1953).

explanation of the child's learning of movement individuation. The child has no background as to associated musculature, little experience in conscious focus of attention on attempts at recognition of movement sensations from a specific body part, and little awareness of how to go about such learning. Yet the child does develop movement individuations as a part of many skills.

SUMMARY

The man of today is bigger, stronger, and more skillful in many physical activities than his counterpart in any preceding generation. This progress is due to man's ability to pass on his experience vicariously to succeeding generations. Health knowledge, especially in nutrition and in the conditioning of the human body, skill forms and procedures, technical knowledge and knowledge of basic mechanics, all have contributed to modern man as a highly developed physical instrument.

Man's behavior is changed, adapted, adjusted, often in progressive hierarchies of advancement, through training and experience. The closest analogy we can draw of the physiological nature of the human organism is the servomechanism and the electronic computer. We do know that we have proprioceptive facilitation with continuous sensory feedback and cord and midbrain servomechanisms. We have large sensory, motor, and association areas in which, apparently, experience is programmed for this human computer. These complex integrative areas seem to develop with experience into higher and higher levels of programming. The data which arrive from the various sense organs are then reassembled in terms of previous experience already programmed into the computer, and response solutions are turned out. The experience accumulated by the individual as life goes on (assuming feedback of results and intent to improve) makes possible finer and finer "computations" and response adjustments.

After infancy one builds his progressing skill complexities on the postural and body-control bases, the simple skills, which he already possesses. This progression, this building on an already learned organization, means that the very nature of the learning process changes. The parts one puts together in maturity already have unique associations and meanings, and the learning is now a strengthening of associations between what are, at this stage, not wholly unrelated activities.

Phylogenetic development (for example, postural controls, eye coordination, reaching and grasping, crawling) does not seem to be greatly accelerated by short periods of special training, but ontogenetic development (for example, using eating utensils, performing toilet routines, buttoning clothes, swimming) seems to be highly dependent on training and experience.

The almost ceaseless bodily activity of the infant, plus whatever innate determinants of the direction of development may exist, seem to insure that the normal youngster will develop most of the muscle contractions (hence movements) he needs for later integration into physical skills. The integration of these movements into a pattern for some purpose is what we mean by motor-skill learning. Two very early examples of simple integration are the child's picking up an object which catches his attention, or his grasping a bottle and holding it to his mouth. It is impossible to separate maturation influence from learning influences in these early stages.

Individuation is the process of learning to divorce body-part performance and control from activities of the whole body. The body part must work over a dynamic or static postural base. Its performance may be (1) over a still base, (2) adjusted to utilize the momentum of a moving base, or (3) adjusted to offset interfering effects of unsuitable body momentum in diverse directions.

Learning to make a new movement not previously under voluntary control involves, first, securing its movement as a part of a gross act; second, gradual practice with attention on the part to be moved and with attempts to relax the other muscles of the gross act; third, practice until the movement occurs as an individuated act with its own "prime-mover" muscle. This extreme type of movement learning is less common in motor learning after infancy but may be needed in the retraining of certain rehabilitation cases, in the precise refinements of certain adjustments requiring a high level of skill, or in the acquirements of certain foreign language pronunciations not present in one's own language.

discussion questions

1. Is modern man an inferior physical specimen to the man of pioneer times in the United States?
2. Are the greater longevity, larger size, and better health of our present generation due directly or indirectly to learning?
3. Does "learning by doing" mean that man only really learns by harsh experience?
4. Can the servomechanisms of the body readjust many actions even after they are under way?
5. Is education a process of building new programs into our "human computers" and supplementing and refining those already recorded?
6. Does "the hierarchical development of skills" imply transfer?
7. Does the infant learn motor skills as rapidly as the adult?
8. Are maturation and learning distinct processes?
9. Does training seem to accelerate phylogenetic development? Ontogenetic development?
10. Does the child *learn* to make the innumerable muscular movements which he performs during infancy?
11. Should one focus his attention on the muscular action when learning a motor pattern? When learning individuation of muscle action?
12. Does the nature of the learning process change from infancy to maturity?

DEFINE:

Learning

Motor Learning

Individuation

II

Factors Affecting
Motor Learning from
Infancy to Old Age

HUMAN LEARNING DIFFERS FROM
ANIMAL LEARNING

The study of psychology often includes animal studies, and we often conclude as to man's behavior from the results found in animal experiments. One famous example is the chicken pecking experiment in which chickens were prevented from pecking at grain and other food during their early days of development.[1] Later on they were compared with chickens who had been allowed intervening experience in pecking. The chickens deprived of the early experience pecked just about as well later on as those who had had the earlier intervening practice. The conclusion is drawn that maturation, rather than learning, produced the precision in pecking. Unfortunately, conclusions as to maturation are often drawn about human learning similar to those drawn from the chicken experiment and other animal development studies. If the human infant had a chicken brain, with its great lack of association areas and its rather limited sensory areas, such analogy might make sense.

Normal youngsters have much more than chicken brains. They need experience to learn most of their adaptations to life. They take on their early primary adaptations much more slowly than do animals, but the possible adaptations available to them are so far beyond the capability of any animal that comparison leads to about as many erroneous conclusions as correct ones. In other words, man's behavior is highly dependent on learning, although the human does indeed need a

---

[1] Charles Bird, "The Effect of Maturation upon the Pecking Instinct of Chicks," *Pedagogical Seminary*, XXXIII:2 (June 1926), 212–34.

great deal of experience in order to acquire his early primary learnings.

> Increase in preschool opportunity to learn motor skills produces greater breadth of interests, more confidence for new ventures, superiority in certain sociomotor skills, better attitudes; and such superiority tends to persist in later years.[2]

Some fourteen years ago the author and a colleague published the preceding statement about value for youngsters of preschool opportunities to learn motor skills. This chapter will consider present thinking about motor-skill training at early ages.

FACTORS AFFECTING RATE AND AMOUNT
OF CHILDHOOD MOTOR LEARNING

At times parents will attempt to foster certain ontogenetic developments which are in immediate demand, such as eating skills and toilet routines. However, several factors tend to cause postponement of more extensive attempts at educating the very young. First, later attempts produce degrees of success which become apparent more quickly because the almost constantly active child has now had more time to acquire postural bases, some eye-hand coordinations, and even a bit more strength as a result of incidental learning. Skills develop in hierarchies, and the higher complexities are more difficult to develop if the component parts (the simpler skills) have not yet been acquired. The lower levels of the hierarchy, the so-called primary learnings of infancy and preschool days, not only take much time to develop but seem to need a much greater quantity of attempts, of trial experiences, before they are acquired.

If the adult attempts to teach a child a skill so complex that adequate postural bases (both static and dynamic) have not yet been acquired, the more complex pattern will develop very slowly, if it is learned at all. Effective methods of teaching change with the level of learning of the learner himself. The methods for the lowest levels require great patience and understanding of both (1) the extra time factor and (2) the quantity-of-experience factor. The youngster will need hundreds of trials over months and months of time.

Jones made an extensive observational study of twenty-four children from the twenty-first through the thirty-third month, then again during the thirty-sixth month and the forty-eighth month. In an analysis of their motor development, she says:

> An integration of the activities began as soon as each activity had reached a stage where all the child's attention was not required in its performance. It seemed that each activity had to become automatic before the child was free to combine activities to any great extent. . . . To a large extent, each activity

---

[2] John D. Lawther and John M. Cooper, "Sub-Committee IV. Methods and Principles of Teaching Physical Education," *56th Annual Proceedings,* The College Physical Education Association (1953), p. 108.

was repeated over and over, without much coordination between the skills involved.[3]

Jones lists as helpful factors in the child's development: a home environment with a playmate one to three years older than the subject, a variety of available play materials, and outdoor play space with opportunity for freedom in locomotor activities. She lists as handicapping factors: a full-time maid, relatives other than the parents living in the home, overprotection by adults, and inhibition in locomotor activities at home.

Brief periods of specialized training of infants by adults have not tended to prove advantageous. Later performance reveals no significant difference between such groups of briefly trained infants and groups without the training. Although relatively limited amounts of practice do not seem to produce permanent superiority, there is some evidence that extensive training does accelerate development. The slowness of early basic learning and the great quantity of experience necessary to produce observable change perhaps account for the findings of such studies. The great amount of incidental learning resulting from the almost constant motor activity of the preschool child greatly overshadows the influence of brief training periods.

Many a fond mother trains her child through iteration and reiteration, day after day and month after month, during these preschool years. Her love for the child, her great concern for his welfare, and her great pride in even his simplest achievements endows her with a patience which is so necessary during this basic learning stage. When she errs, it is usually either by overprotectiveness, too much help, and therefore furthering of dependence; or exasperation with his slow rate of learning, harshness, and therefore inhibition. The fine line between adequate care and guidance by the parent and enough freedom for exploration and self-dependence by the child is difficult to determine. The neglected child may progress rapidly in some types of motor development as a result of the necessity for self-help, but at the same time he may lose out in his social and emotional development.

INFANT TRAINING OF JOHNNY AND JIMMY

Thirty years ago Myrtle McGraw published the results of her much quoted study of the twins, Johnny and Jimmy,[4] and four years later a follow-up study of the same twins appeared.[5] She was attempting to determine the effect of early training on motor-skill development. Johnny, from the age

---

[3] Theresa D. Jones, *The Development of Certain Motor Skills and Play Activities in Young Children,* Child Development Monograph No. 26, Arthur T. Jersild, ed. (New York: Bureau of Publications, Teachers College, Columbia University, 1939), pp. 66–67; pp. 149–50.

[4] Myrtle B. McGraw, *Growth: A Study of Johnny and Jimmy* (New York: Appleton-Century-Crofts, 1935).

[5] Myrtle B. McGraw, "Later Development of Children Specially Trained During Infancy: Johnny and Jimmy at School Age," *Child Development,* X:1 (March 1939), 1–19.

of twenty-one days up to twenty-two months, was subjected to an environment highly stimulating to vigorous and varied activity. He was given daily opportunity and encouragement to engage in both phylogenetic and ontogenetic types of activities—*i.e.*, stimuli to various kinds of mobility such as ascending and descending inclined planes, getting on and off pedestals, playing with multiple sticks, manipulating graded stools and boxes, jumping, tricycling, swimming, and skating.

Jimmy, in the meantime, was given no specific training and spent most of his time in his crib. At the age of twenty-two months Jimmy was introduced to the various activities which Johnny had already experienced. He was given highly stimulating training in those activities in whch he was less skilled than Johnny. After two-and-a-half months of training, Jimmy had approached Johnny's level of skill although he never quite attained it. In the follow-up study four years later, their differences were not great, but Johnny still exhibited greater self-confidence and superior ease and skill.

The age at which Johnny acquired various skills is worth noting. By the age of eight months he was swimming seven feet. At fourteen months he was swimming fifteen feet with his face submerged and was jumping from a height of five feet. He had been started on roller skates at the age of 350 days and at the age of 694 days had acquired reactions which "consisted primarily of the broad rhythmical sway which is characteristic of a proficient skater." [6]

Two or three of McGraw's statements call attention to certain aspects of the effects of preschool training which are well worth considering. With regard to the skating ability of Johnny *before he was two years old* McGraw says:

> ... the skating ability is so outstandingly beyond that of any other child of corresponding chronological age that it would be impossible to deny the influence of daily exercise or repetition of performance upon the development of a specific skill of this type.[7]

With regard to the effect of training on the so-called phylogenetic activities, McGraw says:

> While use of the activity will not advance appreciably the day a child begins to walk alone and will not alter the general method of progression, exercise may influence the grace with which he steps, his speed and his mien of progression.[8]

One other point which relates to specificity of training and transfer is worth quoting here because of its implications. McGraw says:

> Although Johnny had enjoyed earlier and more extensive practice in certain activities, he apparently was not greatly benefited thereby in the acquisition of performances of a different order; *i.e.*, when the gross movement patterns

---

[6] McGraw, *Growth: A Study of Johnny and Jimmy,* p. 163.

[7] *Ibid.,* p. 167.

[8] *Ibid.,* p. 119.

were quite dissimilar to those in the early training, Johnny's advantage disappeared.[9]

This study has been challenged in various ways, including the question as to whether or not the twins were fraternal instead of identical, hence could be expected to be as unlike as brothers and sisters (mere siblings). Nevertheless, it does call attention to the very early age at which the infant can learn relatively complex motor skills, and does thereby raise serious question as to many of the traditional concepts of readiness.

SOME CURRENTLY POPULAR HYPOTHETICAL CONCEPTS OF CHILD DEVELOPMENT

Various hypotheses have been advanced as to ways to facilitate the development of the infant and young child, particularly with reference to the retarded child or the slow learner. The Domans and Delacato from the Institute for Achievement of Human Potentials in Philadelphia hypothesize that reading readiness depends on "complete neurological organization," properly fostered by the correct sequence of infant developmental motor activity. Delacato proposes that reading difficulty can be treated by proper developmental physical exercise, programmed in terms of the gaps which, he hypothesizes, have occurred in the normal sequence of infant motor development; and that reading difficulty can be prevented from occurring in the primary years if such treatment has been adequately administered in the preschool years. He classifies the causes of "inadequate neurological organization" under three headings: (1) genetic, (2) trauma, and (3) lack of environmental opportunity for complete neurological organization. Delacato believes that 70 per cent of those suffering from inadequate neurological organization belong in the last category and that his treatments will be greatly helpful to most of them.

Dr. Temple Fay, in his discussion of treatment of spastic types of paralysis, described the type of prescribed exercise treatments, which was later expanded and used extensively in the Institute for Achievement of Human Potentials. He emphasized the Recapitulation Theory and said:

> ... The patterns of the past lie far below the cortex and, when this higher level is afflicted, may emerge through proper reflex stimulation to give the crude elements of movement and of power that prevailed before the cerebral hemispheres developed.[10]

Dr. Fay described the crawling-pattern exercises utilized in the subject's development as progressing from the homolateral, prone, belly-down crawling to the "crossed diagonal pattern" of creeping. He advocated a program of neuromuscular therapy based on man's evolutionary past—an application

---

[9] *Ibid.,* p. 280.
[10] Temple Fay, "Origin of Human Movement," *American Journal of Psychiatry,* CXI (March 1955), 648.

of the values of "reflex movement" or proprioceptive playback to stir up and utilize the basic primordial patterns on which, he hypothesized, man's later development was based.[11]

Delacato says he diagnoses the child by examining sequential stages of its infant development. In the reeducation procedure Delacato has the child start back at the developmental level which he diagnoses as having been the period at which inadequacies arose; he then programs the child's treatment to have it put through rather intense training in the precise pattern—ranging from prone, belly-down, homolateral crawling to cross-pattern creeping on hands and knees, for example—until the child has mastered each stage to the doctor's satisfaction. He also stresses training for dominance of one side of the body only—handedness, footedness, and eyedness. Some of his theories are:

1. The necessity for hemispheric dominance;
2. The recapitulation theory (ontogeny recapitulates philogeny);
3. A specific organization of the brain with localization of brain function;
4. The great dependence of later intellectual growth on early motor development.

Many objections have been raised to the theoretical basis which Delacato presents for his work. One of the better analyses is that presented in the 28th Yearbook of the Claremont Graduate School Curriculum Laboratory, Claremont, California, 1964, pp. 119–31, edited by Malcolm P. Douglass. In the preceding Yearbook (1963), Carl Delacato presented his viewpoints under the title "The Ontogeny of Reading Problems" (pp. 119–25).[12] In the 28th Yearbook, under the title "Delacato in Review," Dr. F. Theodore Perkins, Professor of Psychology at the Graduate Center, first presents "Problems Arising from Assertions of Assumptions of Delacato." Then Dr. Leon Oettinger, Director of the Department of Electroencephalography at St. Luke Hospital, Pasadena, discusses "The Theory from the Standpoint of Pediatrics." Finally, Dr. William J. Hudspeth, Laboratory of Psychobiology, Claremont Graduate School, discusses "The Neurobehavioral Implausibility of The Delacato Theory." Let us examine some of the points made in these studies.

The hemispheric dominance theory was proposed by Orton and Travis in 1929–30 at Iowa; it was later abandoned when training for this dominance did not result in expected improvement. Longitudinal studies of children have indicated that the recapitulation theory is not an accurate description of child development. Franz and Lashley long ago exploded the "localization of brain function" theory; [13] and most of the more recent studies of the physiology of motor learning have indicated no such hierarchical organization as Delacato describes. There is not much evidence that early motor

---

[11] *Ibid.*, pp. 649–50.

[12] See also C. H. Delacato, *The Diagnosis and Treatment of Speech and Reading Problems* (Springfield, Illinois: Charles C. Thomas, 1963).

[13] See also Henry E. Garrett, *Great Experiments in Psychology* (New York: Appleton-Century-Crofts, 1930), Chap. 14.

development is *predictive* of later intellectual development. Finally, there are many ambidextrous people who show no evidence of any mental retardation—in fact, many who are intellectually brilliant.

Two studies on "creeping, laterality, and reading" were completed by Melvin P. Robbins. The first, his doctoral study at the University of Chicago, was reviewed in *Rehabilitation Literature,* XXVII: 7 (July 1966), 210–11, #454; the second was reviewed in the October issue of the same magazine (#674). In the October issue the problem is attacked thus:

> Both [studies] tested certain relations between neurological organization and reading in the light of Delacato's theory; the primary question is whether evidence gathered in a systematic and controlled manner supports the postulated relationship between reading and creeping, as well as that between reading and laterality.

Findings of neither study gave any support to Delacato's theory. Robbins questions seriously the scientific basis of such a theory.[14]

On the other hand, The Philadelphia Institute of the Domans and Delacato does seem to produce some successes with children who have not been helped by traditional types of treatment. Perhaps Delacato's greatest contribution is the interest he has stirred up with respect to improvement of the greatly retarded child, although there are many other sources of great stimulation in this direction. Perhaps Delacato's successes are in part due to the greatly increased amount of stimulation, care, and affection which is lavished on these children—particularly, to the very great increase in quantity and variety of sensory input and sensory-motor experience which these children obtain under his programming. This latter point is discussed at greater length in this chapter, later under the heading "Quantity of Experience is Very Important in Childhood Learning."

Newell C. Kephart has done considerable work in the area of retarded children and has presented the theoretical background for his procedures.[15] He stresses particularly what he calls the gross motor bases which the child must learn first. He theorizes that the young child goes through a very definite sequence of perceptual-motor learning, and that all subsequent more complex learning is built on these early learning experiences. Starting with early *learning* to sit up and to hold the head up, the child progresses to differentiation (called individuation in this text; see pp. 7–8, 11) such as wrist and finger movements of grasping and picking up objects. Kephart cites previous sources which state that posture is the basic movement pattern out of which all other movement patterns must develop. He thinks that the center gravitational line in one's posture is the zero point for direction, space orientation, and movement.

His concept of laterality and its development is quite different from that of the Delacato dominance hypothesis. Kephart wants the child to experience

---

[14] See also Melvin P. Robbins, "A Study of the Validity of Delacato's Theory of Neurological Organization," *Exceptional Children,* XXXII:8 (April 1966), 517–23.

[15] Newell C. Kephart, *The Slow Learner in the Classroom* (Columbus, Ohio: Charles E. Merrill Books, Inc., 1960); and *The Brain Injured Child in the Classroom* (National Society for Crippled Children and Adults, Inc., 2023 W. Ogden Ave., Chicago, Ill., 1963).

adequate types of learning situations so that the body (not necessarily at the level of conscious awareness) learns to respond with its appropriate parts— arms, legs, hips, or whatever; right or left or with limbs from both sides, as the exigencies of the situation demand. In other words, the individual must develop a *body sense* of laterality, of right and left, just as he must develop a body sense of up and down and of backward and forward.

Perceptual organization develops to some degree along with the individual's motor patterns and continues to develop a little later. In other words, the infant develops a quantity of body knowledge (of motoric knowledge or adaptation, as it were) which is matched later with his perceptual experience. The eyes learn to move together and follow the hand until eye-hand directional kinesthesis is developed. Directionality develops from (1) movements of the limbs out from the center of the body toward objects, (2) movement of the body toward objects, (3) the turning of the eyes to follow hand movements, and (4) the matching of the ocular kinesthesis of this eye movement toward an object with hand contact of the object. Later pursuit games bring on higher levels of this directional development. The progressive matching of motor activity and visual (or auditory) perception develops into space orientation.

Kephart says that the body image is the point of origin of all spatial relationships of objects outside the body. The motor activities of the child teach him "awareness of his body in space and what it can do." Kephart therefore advocates a series of activities through which the motor bases of the backward child may be developed. According to his hypothesis, the proper development of these motor bases will accelerate all the child's later learning, including his academic learning. In brief, Kephart's listed activities include (1) much chalkboard training to develop eye-hand laterality and directionality; (2) much sensory-motor exercise—balance boards, trampoline, "Angels-in-the-Snow," stunts, games, rhythms; (3) form perception training—puzzles, stick figures, peg boards.

It would take too much space here to describe Kephart's proposed developmental program adequately, but we should note that regardless of one's acceptance or rejection of his theories of education, his activity program seems to hold much of value for the *physical* development of the child who is greatly retarded in these motor abilities.

Kephart developed a Perceptual-Motor Survey which purported to determine areas of weakness in the perceptual-motor development of children. The Survey consists of thirty items divided into eleven subtests, with each subtest purporting to measure some particular aspect of the individual's motor development. In 1962 Roach completed a doctoral study at Purdue University in which he attempted to establish the reliability and validity of the Survey.[16] Roach compared scores made on Kephart's Scale by 200 normal children from the first through the fourth grades, with a group of *referrals* in the school system who were normal in intelligence but who had been referred to The Achievement Center for Children at Purdue University as

---

[16] Eugene G. Roach, "The Perceptual-Motor Survey: Normative Study" (Ann Arbor, Michigan: University Microfilm, Inc., 1963).

nonachievers. Roach reported that 85 per cent of the nonachievers scored below 65 on the Survey Scale, while 83 per cent of the control group from the regular classes scored above 65.

In 1964 Little completed a study of the same Scale in which he compared the Survey Scale scores of 103 children with IQs ranging from 50 to 79, all of whom had been approved for the special education program of the Indianapolis Public Schools, with a control group of like ages from the regular classes. He found no statistically significant differences in mean total Survey Scale scores between the educable mentally retarded children and normal children of approximately the same chronological ages. He said that the proposed cut-off point of 65 on the Survey Scale did not differentiate the two groups.

Little did find significant differences on five subtests—namely, jumping, identification of body parts, imitation of movements, Kraus-Weber scores, and "Angels-in-the-Snow." Little's findings of significant differences in the scores of the respective groups on some items are to be expected, as many other studies have reported positive though low correlations between aggregates of physical measurements and mental ability, particularly at the lower end of the intelligence scale.[17]

One must keep in mind, however, that concomitant variation is not necessarily a cause-effect relationship. One would need different evidence before assuming that motor development produced academic aptitude. The problem is a difficult one. Perceiving just what to do in the physical situation (grasping the idea) may be as much a mental as a physical activity, even in as simple an act as child imitation of parent motor act. On the other hand, many of the mental tests have physical performance aspects, particularly for the lower age levels—the cutting with the tiny shears in the Stanford Revision of the Binet-Simon Test, for example. Moreover, some of the experts using the so-called motor aptitude tests (Lincoln Revision of the Oseretsky, for example) have reported that such tests involve certain intellectual weightings. When the question of this weighting is added to the criticism of the degree to which these tests are valid instruments for motor aptitude prediction, then the problem of individual diagnosis and prescription becomes even more difficult. Of course, it is possible that all we are doing in our attempts at analysis is proposing a false dichotomy of mind and body when the two aspects are inseparable in terms of the young child's learning experience. With respect to the intellectual development of the preschool child, Bruner stated that the first stage

> ... consists principally in establishing relationships between experience and action; his concern is with manipulating the world through action. This stage corresponds roughly to the period from the first development of language to the point at which the child begins to manipulate symbols.[18]

[17] Henry Allan Little, "Perceptual-Motor Characteristics of Educable Mentally Retarded Children" (unpublished Doctoral thesis, University of Indiana, 1964).

[18] Jerome S. Bruner, *The Process of Education* (Cambridge: Harvard University Press, 1961), p. 34.

The reader should compare the foregoing discussion of Kephart's theories with the earlier discussion of learning changes from infancy to maturity in Chapter I (see pp. 5–10). With regard to the development of early learning patterns, Hebb says, "It is reasonable to suppose in general that, the less familiar the situation or the task to be performed, the more important slow-increment learning becomes." [19] As we have seen (p. 13), T. Jones calls attention to the fact that each act must become automatic before the child can combine activities.

READINESS

Jones's analysis throws some light on the idea of "readiness"—*i.e.*, lower levels of sensory-motor and perceptual skills must be automatized before the child is ready for the next stage. About the only evidence we have as to readiness is the *average age* at which previous children have shown interest and attacked with success a particular learning area. Some longitudinal studies have attempted to list the basic developments which are essential before the next stage can be attacked successfully, and a few tests or scales to check readiness have been attempted, but there is such a wide individual variability that prediction from averages has little value. In many fields (reading, motor skills) we are finding that the child may be "ready" long before the previously assumed age of readiness. Hereditary factors may cause difference in age of readiness. Richness of environmental experience seems to be a very important factor. The child's interest, upon exposure, is a very important determinant. Attempts to force learning on the very young child before necessary bases are developed may actually cause an emotional block to later learning. However, we tend to err more in postponement than in starting too soon, particularly in motor skills. The degree of the child's own interest and attention span is one of the best cues.

This trend toward lowering the age level at which "readiness" is assumed is becoming very apparent in the academic field; for example, there is a trend now to move the study of languages, science, and mathematics to much younger ages. With regard to the introduction of the basic notions of science and mathematics even as early as the primary grades, Bruner says, "There is no reason to believe that any subject cannot be taught to any child at virtually any age in some form." [20]

The whole concept of readiness needs to be clarified, for a misunderstanding of this concept has often delayed and perhaps retarded motor development in children. In analyzing early learning in terms of readiness, we must keep in mind the quantitative aspect of the process of motor learning; and we must pay special attention to the large amount of incidental learning and its great importance in motor development. Perhaps the children are

---

[19] D. O. Hebb, *Organization of Behavior* (New York: Science Editions, Inc., 1961), p. 115.

[20] Bruner, *op. cit.*, p. 47.

"ready" for the particular types of motor development but the unit of learning with which they are started is too complex for their present level of hierarchical skill development. One is not ready to attempt fielding in the simplest baseball game until he has learned to throw and catch. However, he may be "ready," and may have been ready a considerable time ago, to learn to throw and catch.

Berelson and Steiner make a generalization about readiness for training which emphasizes not only the relative decrease in efficiency of too early training but also the loss of some degree of effectiveness of training postponed after readiness arrives. They say:

> In the learning of complex skills or other abilities requiring training, practice is more effective at the point of maturation—not before, but also not long after, the period of biological readiness.[21]

In the attempts to understand the young child's learning and to foster it or improve its rate, four points stand out from the various observational and experimental studies. They are: (1) what seems to be a very slow rate of progress in primary or sensory-motor learning; (2) the need to automatize each activity before it can be integrated with another activity for a higher stage of learning; (3) the great number of experiences (the quantity of experience) necessary for primary learnings; and (4) the importance of motor experience—manipulating and exploring—as a *means* to learn intellectually as well as physically.

The first point, the slowness of the infant's sensory-motor learning, is perhaps one of the causes of much of the traditional teaching about readiness. It is perhaps illogical to conclude that just because a child learns more slowly at a certain age, he is therefore not ready to learn. The adult learns many things faster than the child chiefly because he has already mastered many of the basic elements and merely needs to integrate them into a more complex hierarchy of learning (see pp. 4–6). Moreover, effective teaching and learning methods are quite different at different levels.

THE QUANTITY OF EXPERIENCE IS
VERY IMPORTANT IN CHILDHOOD LEARNING

The life of a child reared in a favorable environment is full of extensive and varied sense experiences, wide and fluctuating interests, and almost incessant activity. He repeats the same activity many, many times in re-occurring explorations. He builds things and takes them apart repeatedly. The sand pile and his little shovel or scoop and bucket furnish many hours of activity. So does his dog, and his own partly imaginative garden. He plays rough with his dad, teases, chases, or wrestles with his brother or sister, climbs and hangs by his legs, moves the furniture all around, pounds with hammer and nails, tries out hoops and balloons, various balls, velocipedes and bi-

---

[21] Bernard Berelson and Gary A. Steiner, *Human Behavior, An Inventory of Scientific Findings* (New York: Harcourt, Brace & World, Inc., 1964), p. 58.

cycles, boats and rafts. With adult encouragement, he learns to swim, to roller-skate or to ice-skate.

Barker and Wright did a study of children's activity by following them around from early morning until late at night and recording their behavior. They found over two thousand different settings in which the children reacted. By sampling techniques, they estimated the total number of behavior objects to which the normal eight-year-old can react as approximately 1,200,000. They found some 2,200 distinct activities involving about 660 different behavior objects during a waking day.[22]

Many observational studies of children report that they repeat, rework, iterate, and reiterate. Parents often notice the same iteration in speech practice of preschool children. When very young, they will repeat or try to repeat the same expression, phrase or sentence over and over until the nonunderstanding adult becomes impatient and orders them to stop. As many as seventy reiteration trials of a word, phrase, or sentence have been conducted in one sequence of such practice by a child.

Apparently a very considerable quantity of experience is essential to many kinds of learning, and single experiences in these types of learning have little effect. Deprivation studies in which subjects are restricted greatly in stimulation have been found to produce rapid deterioration of function.[23] Apparently the organism needs a certain level of stimulation just to maintain normality and a great deal more to produce permanent change. John Anderson has hypothesized that the child's learning is due chiefly to "a high input and a high outgo," a flow of stimulation and response in which

> ... single experiences or elements occupy relatively insignificant parts. What determines behavior are the relative proportions of different types of stimulation and the amount of reinforcement that occurs.[24]

PHYSICAL EDUCATION AT SCHOOL REPRESENTS
ONLY A SMALL FRACTION OF MOTOR-LEARNING TIME

The time factor, insofar as it involves the quantity-of-experience factor, is often overlooked. The normal preschool child seems to be vigorously active in physical play eight or more hours every day. The elementary school child, if unrestricted by parents or other adult controls, will engage in physical play before school in the mornings, at noon, after school in the evenings, most of Saturday and Sunday, with greatly increased amounts of activity during holidays and vacations. Compare this quantity of ex-

---

[22] Roger G. Barker and Herbert F. Wright, *Midwest and Its Children: The Ecology of an American Town* (Evanston, Illinois: Row, Peterson & Co., 1955), p. 532.

[23] W. H. Bexton, W. Heron, and T. H. Scott, "Effects of Decreased Variation in the Sensory Environment," *Canadian Journal of Psychology,* VIII:2 (June 1954), 70–76; Donald O. Hebb, *A Textbook of Psychology* (Philadelphia: W. B. Saunders Co., 1958), p. 276.

[24] John E. Anderson, "Growth and Development Today: Implications for Physical Education" (Paper presented at National Conference on Social Changes and Implications for Physical Education and Sports Recreation, Estes Park, Colorado, June 1958).

perience of the active youngster with the amount of activity time in the school program of physical education. The "best programs" devote fifty to sixty minutes per day, five days per week, to physical education. Getting to and from class, showering, and dressing take up a part of this time each day. The student is fortunate if he gets forty minutes of class activity per day for five days each week. This amounts to three hours and twenty minutes, yet he will play at something, active or sedentary in nature, for longer than this outside of school on school days. Saturday will double the amount, and Sunday will also double the amount. In other words, the school time can only become really effective if it encourages, fosters, and even directs (permissive, not obligatory) much of the outside-of-school time.

Controlled outside-of-school play, tag, hopscotch, all types of pursuit games, ropes to jump, apparatus to climb and to swing on, mats for tumbling or wrestling, swimming and skating, dancing and team games, plus opportunities to use facilities under guidance, will foster the child's development. He needs encouragement and guidance from intelligent, interested, and able parents, from recreation and playground supervisors, and from teachers through unorganized and organized extracurricular programs. Community planners must arrange for space and equipment, especially with regard to the more complex skills—skating, swimming, badminton, tennis, team games. Gymnastics with apparatus seems to have more appeal at the younger ages than in the late teens, as does track, although supervision and guidance without pressure or forcing is needed. The appropriate activities will vary with the climate and with the sport skills employed by the adults of the community. Children like to imitate adults, and most youngsters will learn much informally by trial and error, and by playing with, observing, and imitating others, peers or adults.

In 1957 Lehman did a study, to expand and follow up a study done in 1954, of the swimming ability of entering college freshmen. In the 1954 study (2,505 subjects), 77 per cent passed the swimming test on entrance to college; in 1957 (2,640 male subjects), 88 per cent passed. Of the sample from the year 1957, 12 per cent could not swim; 4 per cent had learned through private instruction; 28 per cent had learned in school or in clubs, camps, Red Cross classes, Y.M.C.A. programs, etc. However, 56 per cent had learned informally; *i.e.*, without any organized or planned instruction. How much informal learning had contributed to the abilities of the other 32 per cent who could swim (and had had some instruction) is unknown.[25]

CHILD'S NEED FOR VARIETY OF
EXPERIENCE, FREEDOM, SELF-DEPENDENCE

The effect of rich environmental experience in bringing about an earlier arrival of readiness, and hence greater progress by the child, calls attention

---

[25] Karlton B. Lehman, "Where Entering Male Freshmen Learned to Swim and Their Ability to Swim" (Master of Education problem, The College of Health and Physical Education, The Pennsylvania State University, University Park, 1957).

to the need for breadth and variety, a broad base, in nursery school and kindergarten programs. Several studies have indicated that children who have had nursery and kindergarten training tend to maintain superiority in elementary school work over other groups of children who seem to be their equivalents in intelligence and social background, but who have not had this school experience before entering first grade. Studies of children with preschool music training have indicated a persistent group superiority in certain aspects of music over those without the preschool training.[26]

Studies comparing higher and lower socioeconomic groups with respect to motor development often report superiority of the lower economic groups in this aspect of development. Even Gesell, who tended to emphasize the importance of maturation in preschool development, reported finding this difference between economic levels. This finding has been reported frequently enough to cause us to question the methods of child motor training in the "economically comfortable" families (although there are many exceptions—the statement is based on group averages). Questions have also been raised about the motor development aspects of current nursery schools and kindergartens.

A study by Gesell and Lord compared nursery school children, paired in other factors but with one of the pair from a home of low and the other from a home of high economic status. The age range of the subjects was thirty-one through fifty-two months. In most types of development, the higher socioeconomic group was superior; but in the motor developments of self-care—ability to wash hands and face, comb the hair, brush the teeth, button clothes, tie shoes, etc.—the lower-class children excelled. The investigators suggested that the skills were learned out of necessity by the low group because their mothers were working away from home during the day.[27]

Williams and Scott, in a study of Negro infants of contrasting socioeconomic backgrounds, reported significantly more acceleration in motor activities by the lower group. They attributed the superiority of the low socioeconomic group to a permissive atmosphere and to the absence of cribs, playpens, high chairs, and similar restrictive equipment.[28]

Similar findings were reported to the author from a recent study of a large American city. The findings were quite disappointing to the school authorities because they had hoped to find higher scores on the various motor-development tests in the schools with better buildings, higher paid

---

26 Arthur T. Jersild, *Training and Growth in the Development of Children,* Child Development Monograph No. 10 (New York: Bureau of Publications, Teachers College, Columbia University, 1932); Ruth Updegraff, L. Heiliger, and J. Learned, "Part III: The Effect of Training upon the Singing Ability and Musical Interests on Three-, Four-, and Five-Year-Old Children," *University of Iowa Studies in Child Welfare,* New Series, I:346 (1938), 83–121.

27 Arnold Gesell and E. E. Lord, "A Psychological Comparison of Nursery School Children from Homes of Low and High Economic Status," *The Pedagogical Seminary and Journal of Genetic Psychology,* XXXIV:3 (September 1927), 339–56.

28 Judith R. Williams and Roland B. Scott, "Growth and Development of Negro Infants: IV. Motor Development and Its Relationship to Child-Rearing Practices in Two Groups of Negro Infants," *Child Development,* XXIV:2 (June 1953), 103–21.

teachers, and what they considered to be superior equipment. The points that were overlooked by the authorities were the differences in restriction, in outdoor play, and in the frequency of necessity for self-care, as well as the absence in the homes of the poor of facilities and equipment for indoor and more sedentary play or entertainment. The poor encountered the frequent necessity for self-care, and were free to play untold hours outdoors in the streets, alleys, or wherever.

School and preschool experiences should be stimulating and should attempt to develop self-reliance and independence of action. Moreover, it should challenge the child. Gutteridge reported after a very extensive study (1,973 children, thirty-one trained observers, a sample taken from fourteen states) that nursery school, kindergarten, and primary school equipment is not adequately challenging and does not provide varying opportunities or adequate stimulation for developing the motor abilities of children.[29]

MOTOR-SKILL LEARNING AMONG PRIMITIVES

Studies of the motor-skill learning of primitive peoples make very clear to us the effect of quantity and variety of childhood experience.

Stumpf and Cozens, in describing the motor skills of the Maori, the Polynesian natives of New Zealand, say:

> Maori children seem to take to water as though it was their natural element, and under favorable circumstances learned to swim as soon as they learned to walk.[30]

In describing the training of the primitive Manus of New Guinea, Margaret Mead says:

> Expecting children to swim at three, to climb about like young monkeys even before that age, may look to us like forcing them; really it is simply a quiet insistence upon their exerting every particle of energy and strength which they possess.
>
> Swimming is not taught: the small waders imitate their slightly older brothers and sisters, and after floundering about in waist-deep water begin to strike out for themselves. Surefootedness on land and swimming come almost together, so that the charm which is recited over a newly delivered woman says, "May you not have another child until this one can walk and swim." [31]

Margaret Mead goes on to explain that mere infants are taught how to maneuver boats of all kinds:

---

29 Mary V. Gutteridge, "A Study of Motor Achievements of Young Children," *Archives of Psychology,* No. 244 (May 1939).

30 Florence Stumpf and Frederick W. Cozens, "Some Aspects of the Role of Games, Sports and Recreational Activities in the Culture of Modern Primitive Peoples," *Research Quarterly,* XVIII:3 (October 1947), 213.

31 Margaret Mead, *Growing Up in New Guinea* (New York: New American Library of World Literature, Inc. [a Mentor Book], 1930), p. 26. Copyright 1930, 1958, by Margaret Mead.

... Early in the morning the village is alive with canoes in which the elders sit sedately on the center platforms while small children of three punt the canoes which are three or four times as long as the children are tall.[32]

There is great insistence on mastery of all physical skills by the child as early in infancy as possible:

The test of this kind of training is in the results. The Manus children are perfectly at home in the water. They neither fear it nor regard it as presenting special difficulties and dangers. The demands upon them have made them keen-eyed, quick-witted, and physically competent like their parents. There is not a child of five who can't swim well. A Manus child who couldn't swim would be as aberrant, as definitely subnormal as an American child of five who couldn't walk.[33]

His whole play world is so arranged that he is permitted to make small mistakes from which he may learn better judgment and greater circumspection, but he is never allowed to make mistakes which are serious enough to permanently frighten him or inhibit his activity. He is a tightrope walker, learning feats which we would count outrageously difficult for little children, but his tightrope is stretched above a net of expert parental solicitude.[34]

In other aspects of adapting the children to the external world the same technique is followed. Every gain, every ambitious attempt is applauded; too ambitious projects are gently pushed out of the picture; small errors are simply ignored but important ones are punished. . . .[35]

... This attitude, severe and unsympathetic as it appears on the surface, makes children develop perfect motor coordination . . . but in the everyday activities of swimming, paddling, punting, climbing, there is a general high level of excellence. And clumsiness, physical uncertainty and lack of poise, is unknown among adults.[36]

Mead explains that physical development and skill is so universal among the Manus that they have no word in their language for clumsiness. They have seen *all* adults finally achieve these great physical skills and proficiencies. The child's lesser proficiency is simply described as "not understanding yet." As a child, he learns all the physical skill necessary for physical adjustment to life. Mead says:

... By a system of training which is sure, unhesitant, unremitting in its insistence and vigilance, the baby is given the necessary physical base upon which he builds through years of imitation of older children and adults. The most onerous part of his physical education is over by the time he is three. For the rest it is play for which he is provided with every necessary equipment, a safe and pleasant playground, a jolly group of companions of all ages and both sexes. He grows up to be an adult wholly admirable from a physical standpoint, skilled, alert, fearless, resourceful in the face of emergency, reliable under strain.[37]

---

[32] *Ibid.,* p. 26.
[33] *Ibid.,* p. 27.
[34] *Ibid.,* p. 25.
[35] *Ibid.,* p. 27.
[36] *Ibid.,* p. 28.
[37] *Ibid.,* pp. 36–37.

EARLY TRAINING AS
RELATED TO POTENTIALITY

Whether or not actual motor-achievement potentiality is increased by more extensive preschool and childhood training is undetermined. Individuals do seem to be able to reach higher final levels, on the average, if they start the developmental practice quite young. Studies of the effects of music training, and nursery and kindergarten training, as well as observations of the developments of children of primitive races, all indicate higher levels of achievement by those who start young. During the last fifty years, the average age of those attaining national and international championships in many sports has dropped about eight years. However, studies of these athletes indicate that the number of years of consistent practice before reaching championship achievement has not changed greatly. The athlete still seems to need eight to ten years of consistent practice to achieve these highest peaks. He just starts younger. Moreover, with continuing motivated practice, excellence of performance continues over many more years than it did formerly. In other words, high skill levels are achieved at much younger ages and often persist as high efficiency of performance to a much more advanced age than was customarily found even a generation ago.

Perhaps the answer is not that potentiality is increased significantly by childhood training, but that potentiality should be fostered at the first appearance of readiness; and may be partially lost if training is postponed until later years. In the generalization by Berelson and Steiner cited above (p. 22) you will note that they said practice was more effective at a point of readiness—"not before, but also not long after. . . ." McGraw was of the opinion that roller-skating could be learned most economically at the stage in which the child "was just beginning to gain equilibratory control." [38] Recent studies have indicated significant positive correlations between various measures of swimming and of balance.[39] Many children of nursery and kindergarten age are now found to have great success in learning to swim. Whether it is a balance factor which makes swimming so easy for these young children to learn, or whether the ability to learn has something to do with the gross muscular nature and total bodily activity of the skill must await further research to determine.

MOTOR SKILL FOUNDATIONS
DIFFICULT TO BUILD AT ADULTHOOD

Let us look for a moment at the other extreme, the bottom percentiles in motor abilities in the required first year of physical education activities of large American universities. (The pressure of enrollments and the cost of facilities for such programs are tending to eliminate this requirement in some

---

[38] McGraw, *Growth: A Study of Johnny and Jimmy,* p. 241.

[39] Elmer A. Gross and Hugh L. Thompson, "Relationship of Dynamic Balance to Speed and to Ability in Swimming," *Research Quarterly,* XXVIII:4 (December 1957), 342–46; John A. Reeves, "A Study of Various Types of Balance and their Relationship to Swimming Endurance and Speed" (unpublished Master of Science thesis, The Pennsylvania State University, 1962).

areas of the U.S.) Several studies have been made of girl students, average age about eighteen, who arrive at the university with very inadequate body control in performing the physical activities common to the social and recreational life of their peers. Many experiments have been tried in attempts to improve this low group in some way. "Significant differences" have been reported in improvement of these groups when placed in special classes and given instruction which seemed to be adaptable to their level of development, as compared to groups of the same level which were admitted to the regular classes of heterogeneous abilities. The improvements of these low groups, even when taught in special classes, are so slight in comparison with the average group, that the differences are greater instead of less after each has had a year of training. Most of the low group never seem to attain enough skill to be welcome participants in the various recreational and sociomotor physical activities of their academic peers. They prefer to be scorekeepers or equipment caretakers during the school period, and learn to avoid this whole area of "little success" for the rest of their lives.

The person who arrives at adulthood with very little development of his body-control, sociomotor, or recreational skills—the so-called "motor illiterate"—rarely has the time, the energy, the patience, or the desire to build those slowly developing bases which were neglected in childhood. The vigorous physical activity of childhood and the hour after hour, day after day, and week after week of play are gone and cannot be resurrected. Social demands, conventional behavior and inhibitions, academic work, one's job, all combine to interfere with any planned skill-development program for the low-skilled adult. Few people have the time to build these slowly developing bases; hence they avoid situations in which they display extreme inefficiency, or they have little interest in practicing activities in which they "lose face" because of the social stigma of incompetency, and in which they are rarely rewarded by significant success.

In 1960 Nessler did a study of college freshman girls who were at the lowest percentile (based on over 1,600 entering freshman girls tested) as measured by various motor-skill tests. She put her experimental subjects in special classes in which the first eight weeks were devoted to practice of basic skills and body-control movements, the area in which these students seemed to be most deficient. The next eight weeks were spent on the fundamentals of badminton. Her control group from the same low percentile was placed in the regular program of required physical education for girls.

The activity abilities which Nessler tried to develop in her low groups included ball handling (throwing, catching, bouncing); striking or batting a ball; running, dodging, and changing direction; jumping; and kicking a ball.

Nessler concluded at the end of her experiment that, although a skills class adapted in program and method to low-skilled students was more advantageous than the regular class for these students in performance of the specific skills practiced, such a skills course could not compensate for their vast lack of experience in motor skills.[40]

---

[40] Joan Nessler, "An Experimental Study of Methods Adapted to Teaching Low-Skilled Freshman Women in Physical Education" (Unpublished Doctoral dissertation, The Pennsylvania State University, 1962).

Docherty made a follow-up study of these same low-skilled students after they had completed their two years of required physical education. She concluded in part as follows:

> Low-motor-skilled students seem to gain in skill and favorable attitude toward physical education from participation in a special activities class adapted to their needs at the specific time of the class; but then seem to gradually retrogress in their skill and attitude as time increases after the culmination of the special class even though they are still continuing to attend physical education classes.[41]

FACTORS LIMITING ADULT MOTOR LEARNING

Whether this inability to attain average performance is completely due to inadequate background, or discouragement through lack of success, or even an emotional block, a complete loss of interest followed by development of compensating activities; or whether it is partially due to some actual loss of potentiality through long postponement of adequate educational experience is not known. The relative lack of success with this low group, even when extra time for practice is arranged and special rewards are made available (and apparently real interest in improvement is aroused), seems to indicate some deterioration in potentiality through long postponement of training. However, one should remember that only in infancy and childhood does one have the many, many hours of time for vigorous physical play, and the excess energy to devote to such activities. Adolescence and adulthood bring on many competing activities of a more sedentary nature, many social inhibitions to vigorous physical play, especially for girls, and many other interests which compete with vigorous physical play.

ADVANCED AGE AND LEARNING

It must not be assumed, however, that average individuals lose much of their ability to learn motor skill after middle age. Normal individuals well beyond middle age can learn motor skills if they want to do so and are not too fearful about trying something new. At first, however, they often lack confidence in their own ability to learn.[42] They tend to be a little slower, a little more cautious, and a bit less keen in their receptor senses.[43] Rapidly paced learn-

---

41 Ethel Docherty, "The Developmental Progress of Low-Skilled College Women in a Required Physical Education Program" (Unpublished Master's thesis, The Pennsylvania State University, 1962).

42 Solomon Barkin, "Redesigning Jobs in Industry for a Maturing Population," *Age Is No Barrier* (Report of the New York State Joint Legislative Committee on Problems of Aging, 1952), pp. 92–96; Pearl Berlin, "The Learning of Swimming by Senior Citizens" (a research project cosponsored by the AUW Recreation Department and Wayne State University, Division of Health and Physical Education, October 20, 1960).

43 Barkin, *op. cit.;* A. T. Welford, *Skill and Age* (London: Oxford University Press, 1951), pp. 121–23; J. A. Williams, "Speed of Movement and Chronological Age" (Unpublished Master's thesis, The Pennsylvania State University, 1958).

ing is harder for them than if they are allowed to set their own pace.[44]

Subjects well beyond middle age present a problem as to methods of teaching them gross physical skills, for they seem to experience difficulty in translating the instructor's demonstrations into their own performance. Manual manipulation often seems to be quite helpful.[45] They should be allowed to progress at their own chosen rate, without pressure.[46] They often find equally successful compensatory changes to substitute for certain impairments.[47] They will need clearer, stronger, and perhaps more frequently repeated cues to give them the idea.[48]

If subjects have health and vigor, motivation, and an average background in physical activity, they can learn many industrial, hobby, or recreational skills of a physical nature, even in the sixth and seventh decades of their lives.[49] Many retired people have learned to swim, skate, ski, or even play racket games. They tend to be somewhat slower, but may become quite accurate.[50] Moreover, such learning activity often has real therapeutic value.[51]

SUMMARY

In general, little formal attempt is made to teach infants and preschool children gross physical skills. The following factors foster this postponement of serious attempts to educate very young children in any motor skills except those which are in immediate demand (eating, toilet training, etc.).

1. Much time and patience are essential for teaching very young children. These early sensory-motor learnings take great quantities of time and great numbers of trial experiences for their very slow development. Children show evidence of more rapid learning after maturation and incidental practice have developed postural bases, eye-hand coordinations, and certain strengths.

2. Methods of teaching older children, especially verbal explanation and description, are not effective at this earlier age.

3. Experimental studies involving brief periods of specialized training of infants by adults tend to reveal no measurable degree of improvement.

4. The fine line between adequate care and guidance by the parent and still enough freedom for exploration and self-dependence by the child is difficult to determine. The necessity for self-dependence has been found to hasten certain motor skill acquirements.

---

44 Welford, *op. cit.;* G. E. W. Wolstenholme and M. P. Cameron, eds., *Aging—General Aspects,* Vol. I of *CIBA Foundation Colloquia on Aging* (Boston: Little, Brown & Co., 1955).

45 Berlin, *op. cit.*

46 Wolstenholme and Cameron, *op. cit.*

47 Frances Hellebrandt, "The Physiology of Motor Learning," *Cerebral Palsy Review,* XIX:4 (July-August 1958), 9–14.

48 Berlin, *op. cit.;* Welford, *op. cit.*

49 Berlin, *op. cit.;* A. J. Carlson, "Education for Later Maturity in the U.S.A.," Report of the Third Congress of the International Association of Gerontology (London: E. & S. Livingston, Ltd., 1955), p. 611.

50 Hellebrandt, *op. cit.*

51 Berlin, *op. cit.*

5. The smallness of the fraction of total motor-learning time represented by the school physical education programs is rarely realized. In almost any day, the healthy child participates in more vigorous activity outside of class than he does in a whole week of physical education classes. Moreover, he often devotes all weekend and most of his holidays to physical activity. What he is permitted, helped, and encouraged to do outside of class can be of much more advantage to him in motor-skill achievement than all the practice within the class activity programs.

6. The traditional concept of "readiness," or lack of it, has tended to postpone too long the child's participation in useful physical activities which he will enjoy, can learn, and will use extensively, once learned.

7. A child needs a wide variety of motor experiences, much freedom, and as much self-dependence as possible without too great personal hazard. Oversupervision and overprotection have proved inhibiting in the area of motor-skill acquirement. The studies of primitive peoples have made very clear the effects of quantity and variety of childhood motor experience.

Early motor-skill training seems to be related to higher peaks of skill achievement in later life. Skill, ability to succeed, more opportunity for the more skilled to participate, growth of interest with increase in skill, all may contribute to superiority in skills as an adult for the child who starts younger. Whether or not potentiality for development is increased by preschool training is not yet clear.

Motor-skill foundations (the simple body-control bases), if lacking, are difficult to build at adulthood because they take so much time to acquire and because discouragement results from lack of success. The adult resents appearing clumsy and awkward, hence loses interest and resorts to compensating activities of a less physical nature. Competing activities of a sedentary nature usually do not permit the adult to devote the time needed for learning the elementary bases of many physical recreational skills. Moreover, society in the United States tends to create social inhibitions to vigorous physical play by adults, especially women.

We often overlook the fact that during infant and preadolescent years the child has almost indefatigable energy. If he is healthy and is not denied the opportunity, he practices various body-control and sociomotor skills almost every waking moment. Moreover, never again will he have available such a great amount of vigorous-activity time. Never again will the child have hour after hour, day after day, and week after week of time to engage in his own play and to pursue his own inclinations toward vigorous activity. As he moves into adolescence, his almost irrepressible energy diminishes somewhat; social demands, assigned duties, school work, conventional behavior and inhibitions, all combine to decrease very greatly the hours of physical activity which characterized his preschool and elementary school years. However, the average adult can learn motor skills if he wants to do so, even well past middle age. As he gets beyond fifty years of age, he tends to be a little slower, may have more difficulty with his receptor senses, and does not learn as well under pressure. With motivation, health, and growth of self-confidence, he can learn to perform many motor skills rather well even into the sixth and seventh decades of his life.

discussion questions

1. Do experiments with animals reveal how man learns?
2. Is the human infant slower in motor learning than many animals?
3. Is it advisable to attempt to train the nursery school child in various types of ontogenetic development?
4. Does integration of simple movement activities into larger patterns begin as soon as the child's attention is not required to focus on performance of the simpler activity?
5. Have brief periods of specialized training of infants tended to produce observable improvement over those not so trained?
6. Is quantity of experience the key to childhood adaptation and adjustment in motor behavior?
7. Are freedom and self-dependence basic factors in more rapid motor development of preschool children?
8. Does the child acquire the major part of his motor development and physical skills in school?
9. Is postponement of training after "readiness" advisable lest we accelerate the child too much?
10. Did Jimmy, in McGraw's study, achieve the same levels as Johnny even though his training came at a later stage of development?
11. Do the lower economic classes tend to be retarded in motor-skill development?
12. Is there great emphasis on motor-skill acquirement in child training among primitive people?
13. May early training increase potentiality?
14. May a great lack of early training make gross motor-skill acquirement unlikely in adulthood?
15. Can an old person who so desires learn new sport skills? Industrial skills?

The Nature
of Learning:
Types and Theories

LEARNING INVOLVES ONE'S ENTIRE BEING

The changes in human behavior resulting from training, experience, or both, and called learning, involve one's entire being. One's learning includes both implicit and overt responses, and includes changes in attitudes, emotions, ideas, concepts and generalizations, motor and verbal responses. Unconscious conditionings are likely to accompany much of our purposeful learning. The individual is a unified organism, not a dichotomy —not a bipartite organism divided into mind and body. In our attempt to classify learning into types according to its major aspects, we are emphasizing only what we can observe in active response. However, various concomitant learnings accompany almost any major objective in learning. I learn skills but at the same time I learn to enjoy or dislike them; to compete and to love competition or vice versa; to be concerned about my physical condition lest I be unsuccessful; to react to social pressures and game rules; to cooperate with my teammates and opponents; to be emotionally stimulated by certain environmental atmospheres; to like certain associates and perhaps dislike others; to be fearful or courageous in critical situations, and so on.

The degree to which the various parts of the human organism participate in learning may well vary along a continuum, but hypothetically no part is ever likely to reach zero activity when other parts of the organism are engaged in learning. There is adequate evidence of much learning which occurs below the level of conscious awareness and involves an involuntary response—as different from purposeful learning as was the conditioning of the iris muscle of the eye to contract at the ringing of a bell, in Hulsey Cason's famous experiment.[1] At the other extreme, there is the inductive-deductive approach of the research scholar in his search for truth; and the design of his experiment may very well involve a very considerable amount of creative imagination, also. Yet the research scholar has attitudes, emotionally toned, which affect his work—his strong conviction that he must rely on factual evidence is an example. William James recommended that one reduce the details of daily life to the custody of automatism so that his mind would be free for higher activities;[2] However, man functions as a unitary organism, and not as two halves—an automaton and a "free" mind. The various parts of the human being do not function independently, even though all aspects do not reach conscious awareness.

A DRIVE OR PURPOSE
BASIC TO LEARNING

In learning, the individual is faced with a situation which stimulates him, raises some tension in him, causes some disequilibrium. Some drive, purpose, or goal is activating him. Completely satiated animals or completely satisfied humans do not strive for further achievement or adaptation. The progress of man seems to depend on this dissatisfaction, this discontent, this striving to satisfy needs. The individual who is completely satisfied and contented makes no progress, makes no attempt to adjust, adapt, learn. According to Hull,[3] responses which reduce need are thereby reinforced but if the response does not reduce need, the response is inhibited. According to him, reinforcement (reward of response with reduced drive following response) causes an organization in the nervous system which links future stimuli and responses in the sequence in which they occurred when the need was reduced.

LEARNING VARIES IN
NATURE AND COMPLEXITY

For the purpose of this text, we have adopted a functional view of the nature of learning, based on what conditions produce what outcomes. Our conclusions are a synthesis of experimentally or empirically derived generalizations, and are eclectic; *i.e.,* they are chosen from various experimental findings without concern for underlying theory. Tolman's suggestion that there are a number of different kinds of learning [4] may be a practical hypothesis

---

[1] Hulsey Cason, "Conditioned Pupillary Reaction," *Journal of Experimental Psychology,* V:2 (April 1922), 108–46.

[2] William James, *Talks to Teachers on Psychology* (New York: Holt, Rinehart and Winston, Inc., 1916).

[3] Clark L. Hull, *Principles of Behavior* (New York: Appleton-Century-Crofts, 1943), pp. 383 ff.

[4] Edward C. Tolman, "There is More Than One Kind of Learning," *Psychological Review,* LVI:3 (May 1949), 144–55.

for us to accept as we study the factors which affect learning, although we should bear in mind that Katona's analysis of the learning of material ranging from pure rote memory to highly organized content indicates a continuity of the learning processes rather than discrete types.[5] Perhaps an eclectic view would accept Tolman's view only as emphasis on the major aspect of the learning, with lesser aspects always accompanying the major emphasis.

Perhaps a look at some of the ways that have been used to describe kinds of learning will help us understand its nature and complexity. Division into kinds or categories is only an artificial division of processes which occur along a continuum, and is done in an attempt to help analysis and understanding.

LATENT LEARNING [6]

In accordance with the stress on incidental learning in Chapter I, I should like to examine first a type of learning often overlooked—namely, latent learning. Learning seems to occur even when the learner has no intention or any particular drive to learn. The word "latent" does nothing to describe the process or nature of such learning; it merely indicates that performance at the time in which the learning must have been taking place gave no evidence of any change. The fact that responses have been modified is evidenced later in faster learning or better performance. Mere association without any intent to learn may contribute to faster learning at some later date if the later association is accompanied by a drive or purpose. Latent learning seems to occur at times although the responses learned were unrewarded.

Perhaps another way to describe latent learning would be to say that the child may be learning, to some degree, if he is just being put through the motions of the act by his parents, even though he has no interest and no desire to learn the particular responses. Curiosity and exploratory activity of the child apparently develop in him an acquaintance with things, certain space orientations, feelings of familiarity, and certain basic perceptual-motor controls—all learnings which have occurred without direct motivation toward them. Hull, who was cited earlier emphasizing the importance of drive in learning, says there is also learning in which no reduction of primary need, by the responses which are learned, takes place. Hull says:

> Careful observation and experimentation reveal, particularly with the higher organisms, large numbers of situations in which learning occurs with no associated primary need reduction.[7]

However, Hull believes that some secondary, associated need may be causing the activity and therefore the learning.

---

[5] George Katona, *Organizing and Memorizing* (New York: Columbia University Press, 1940).

[6] Cf. Donald Thistlewaite, "A Critical Review of Latent Learning and Related Experiments," *Psychological Bulletin*, XLVIII:2 (March 1951), 97–129.

[7] Hull, *op. cit.*, p. 387.

LEARNING THROUGH CONDITIONING

Since the time of Pavlov's famous conditioning experiments in which he substituted the ringing of a bell for meat powder as a stimulus to saliva flow in dogs, numerous conditioning experiments have been carried out with both animals and humans. By arranging conditions so that an unconditioned (original) stimulus is contiguous with a neutral stimulus, one will eventually teach the animal to produce the unconditioned response whenever the neutral stimulus is present. This type of involuntary-response conditioning has been called "classical conditioning."

In addition to the many animal conditioning experiments, numerous experiments of this type have been conducted with humans; *e.g.*, conditioning of eyelid blink, galvanic skin-response, bladder control (conditioned to waken) of bed-wetting infants, patellar tendon response, and various vasomotor responses. These experiments very well demonstrate the type of learning in humans which is called involuntary response conditioning—learning which occurs without conscious awareness by the subject of the change which is taking place, except insofar as he observes his own conditioned behavior after the change. Many an old athlete experiences an acceleration of heart rate when he hears a band playing the same tunes played by bands years before as he was preparing to start certain varsity football games during his undergraduate days. The response is involuntary and was learned unconsciously. Many of our feelings, our emotions, our superstitions are changes which have occurred in us because of this type of learning.

Watson conditioned various infants to fear a rabbit by making its appearance to the infant contiguous with the occurrence of a loud noise behind the child's ear. Watson extended his experiments and based his whole psychological theory of the nature of learning, Behaviorism, on a conditioned-reflex hypothesis. This theory was very popular in the third decade of this century, and persisted until Franz and Lashley established a theory of the somewhat generalized functioning of the brain (as opposed to Watson's theory of function by established reflex arcs) through their brain-part extirpation experiments with primates and lower animals.

Mothers often condition their children to fear various things either by frightening statements or by revealing their own fears. We acquire innumerable conditions through incidental learnings. The sight, smell, or verbal description of food often causes salivary flow in a hungry person, revealed perhaps through a number of swallowing acts. How many conditionings of this type become patterned into our daily behavior is difficult to estimate but apparently the amount is large. Children often become conditioned to react according to certain attitudes in the classroom, to others on the playground, to still others when adult company visits their home. Such conditionings are often relatively permanent. Old books, pennants, pictures, or other mementos of one's undergraduate days often arouse a feeling of nostalgia, years later.

Much learning is the substitution of a contiguous stimulus for the original stimulus because of the temporal association of the two stimuli. Contiguity of the stimuli during some repetitions of the activity causes an adaptation in which the unconditioned stimulus may be replaced by a conditioned stimulus. Higher order conditioning may involve the substitution of words as conditioned stimuli. I learn to attach a word to the food I want by association. Later I may substitute another conditioned stimulus for this one; *e.g.*, milk, *lait, leche, milch, etc.* This temporal learning through association occurs with both involuntary and voluntary responses. Let us progress to types of learning involving voluntary responses and purposeful attempts at learning.

TRIAL AND ERROR

Perhaps the next classification along the continuum of learning is what Thorndike has called "trial-and-error learning." In this type of learning, the individual is faced with a situation in which he wants to do something but does not know how to go about it. He has a drive, a motive, a purpose, a need, or a desire. He tries out various responses, guiding himself as best he can from past experience, but rather blindly if the situation is quite novel. He gradually discards the unsuccessful types of activity and adopts those which seem to bring him closer to his goal. With continued practice, he discards much of the extraneous activity, and integrates into a pattern those activities which lead to his goal. Trial and error is quite characteristic of your behavior when you attempt to learn a completely new skill, although imitation of others helps you in your selection of provisional tries.

If the subject has some background in the relevant area but does not know the specific approach to his new goal, he may very well rehearse many of the activities mentally, discarding some of them as ineffective without expressing them overtly. In other words, there is a more sophisticated type of trial and error in which many of the tries are only mental rehearsals.

BOND FORMATION

Thorndike's theory of bond formation, $S \xrightarrow{\text{(bond)}} R$, and his emphasis on learning being the strengthening of bonds between stimuli and following responses which were satisfying, has had a great influence on educational practice. The teacher arranges the learning situation so that the students are more likely to make the responses which are satisfying to themselves; of course, the environment is arranged so that these responses are also those desired by the teacher. The student has a goal toward which he may have already been stimulated by parent or teacher influence. He tries out responses which he thinks will help him toward that goal. For faster learning he should experience early successes (reinforcements of responses through law of effect), and more successes than failures. Such success implies teacher guidance as to goals, teacher organization of the learning environment, and encouragement.

Thorndike's association theory is now often classified as a type of conditioning based on the principle of reinforcing the associative bond between the stimulus and the desired response. The desired response, when it occurs, is rewarded, thereby strengthening the bond. Failure to reward a response repeated several times is the procedure for eliminating that response.

Research has indicated that both rewarding the correct response and punishing the incorrect response may hasten the strengthening of the desired response. However, the results of studies on the effect of making a wrong response annoying (by means of punishment) in order to eliminate it are somewhat conflicting. Severe punishment seems at times to be deleterious to learning even when applied only to incorrect responses. In some few instances mild punishment may be helpful (mild shock, for example) even if it is applied to the correct response. The causal factor seems to be the attention getting value of the mild shock to furnish information, playback, as to success. Attention is called to success and the reward of the success now attended to, more than compensates for the mild punishment. Information as to success seems to be very important in facilitating learning. Perhaps this is just another way of saying that one will endure a bit of annoyance if he sees that the satisfaction of his wants is thereby being attained; *i.e.,* the reward more than compensates for the punishment.

Information about degree of success, playback of exact results, and encouragement ("good," "correct," "well done," "fine progress," etc.), all seem to be effective factors in strengthening responses, in favoring the establishment of these responses over those not so reinforced. Throwing or shooting at a target has an instant playback of results; the subject sees immediately his degree of success. A larger target and a shorter distance for the novice permit a higher degree of information playback because he needs to hit the target somewhere in order to see just how far he hit off center.

The continuum of learning from the nonvoluntary-response type of classical conditioning through trial and error (Thorndike's connectionism) up to the functioning of the highest level of thought, all seem to have association of stimuli with stimuli, and stimuli with responses, by contiguity of occurrence and response reinforcement (reward). Moreover, learning involves attitudes, emotions, and various physiological reactions, whether one is attempting to acquire physical skills or academic learning. We have considered the listed types of learning as change-phenomena occurring along a continuum in which the same basic principles apply—drive, contiguity of stimuli, and responses which are satisfying in result.

INSIGHT LEARNING;
THE GESTALT OR FIELD THEORY

In the mental "trial-and-error" process, we seem at times to "hit upon" a quick solution. One whole school of psychology stresses this process of "suddenly hitting upon" a suitable response. The Gestalt theory of learning emphasizes the reorganization of the total stimulus situation by one's mind into a meaningful unit or pattern (a Gestalt). An analogy to the Gestaltist's concept of the reorganization of environmental stimuli received from a situation is provided by the transformation which occurs to produce a stereophonic sound melody as it is organized and transmitted to the human ear from a vinyl disc. The interpreting done by the record player and accompanying apparatus is analogous to the reorganization done within one's being, and the vinyl disc with its indentations is analogous to the external stimulus situation.

External stimuli furnish, as we relate and organize them, cues which fuse into meanings. The Gestalt psychologist assumes that the complex of stimuli arriving through the senses is being constantly organized and interpreted into units of meanings (Gestalts); and that this organizing, this development of insight, is learning. The Gestaltist, however, in addition to his consideration of the mind as a transforming, unifying system, stresses *the sudden emergence* of meaning in contrast with the gradual adjustment of the association theory. Köhler used as the criterion of insight *"the appearance of a complete solution with reference to the whole layout of the field."* [8]

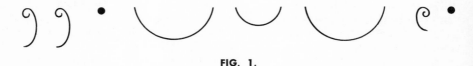

FIG. 1.

The Gestaltist says that the whole stimulus situation is organized in terms of figure and background; and the perception, the meaning, the insight comes from the whole pattern, the unified pattern. The organization provides more than just an aggregation of parts. The very organization in itself adds the meaning. Look at the illustrations below in Figures 1, 2, and 3. Figure 1 is just an aggregate of dots and curved lines. Figure 2 presents exactly the same lines and dots but reorganized into a pattern. Figure 3 is the same as Figure 2 except for the inversion of one curved line, yet the meaning changes.

FIG. 2.

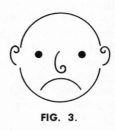

FIG. 3.

The constituent parts of these figures are identical but the arrangement, the relationship of parts in space, has caused a reorganization of perception—has added meaning. The Gestalt theory emphasizes that the decision on appropriate activity, the solution to problems in a situation which then flows into overt activity by the subject, comes about as the subject "sizes up" the situation and "hits upon" an appropriate response. He has reorganized the incoming stimuli into a meaningful Gestalt. Learning is the reorganization of perceptions and adjustment of responses through these insights.

---

[8] Wolfgang Köhler, *The Mentality of Apes* (New York: Harcourt, Brace & World, Inc., 1925), p. 190.

is insight learning merely highly sophisticated mental trial and error?

The trial-and-error advocate would say that in Köhler's well-known experiment, the ape Sultan may have tried out some procedures mentally before he went for the box to climb on to reach the fruit.[9] However, so-called insight learning does seem to occur to most people at times. They seem to suddenly "hit upon" a solution mentally, then carry out the conceived idea. It may be that the difference is merely the extent to which the unsuccessful "provisional tries" occur below the level of conscious awareness, if we accept the hypothesis of some reorganization at a subconscious level. We do seem to have ideas which arrive at the level of conscious awareness rather well organized—in fact, so well developed that they often burst forth as an overt expression. Sometimes (perhaps too rarely) we are amazed, or at least delighted, at how cleverly we have expressed an idea after we have spoken "on the spur of the moment"; and sometimes we are disturbed that we should have burst forth with so stupid a statement. In each case, we have expressed the thought without first rehearsing it consciously.

Most analyses of the nature of creative imagination state three basic aspects of the process: (1) acquisition of an extensive background in the content area (of the creation); (2) a period of relaxation (incubation) without awareness-level consideration of the problem, although the drive and interest in the whole problem area may be just beneath conscious focus, and may be undergoing some change; then (3) the sudden insight which may be released in its newly organized form by almost any extraneous cue from the environment.

Many a coach keeps cards in his pocket, or on the lampstand beside his bed at night, to record sudden ideas (insights?) which "pop into" his mind. Some few of these "sudden insights" prove to be ingenious ideas after being tried out in practice, but many turn out to be of no value when submitted to the test of team scrimmage. The mature adult tends to use mental "trial-and-error" in an attempt to save time, and perhaps the embarrassment or even cost of overt expression of the "errors." Problem solving could very well be considered a form of mental "trial and error." When a solution does come to mind, is this insight? As the human mind reduces more and more of its experience to the shorthand of verbal and mathematical symbolism, a much more sophisticated type of implicit activity, of mental overview of the problem and of weighing the evidence, can take place. Solutions are more likely to be rapid. Hypothetical solutions or ideas of action will "come to mind" out of a wealth of experiential background stored somewhere in one's memory drums. However, this type of attempt to achieve a purpose or to restore equilibrium to a stimulated nervous system, is just the upper end of the continuum of the learning processes which extend all the way down to activity of the simple classical-conditioning type. In terms of the computer analogy, learning at advanced levels is much different because

---

[9] *Ibid.*

so much usable adjustment is already programmed into the computer. (Hebb's statement quoted above, p. 6, presents somewhat the same view.)

applications of the Gestalt theory

We must not overlook the Gestaltists' emphasis on meaningfulness. Meaning is certainly very helpful in learning, retention, and application of knowledge. In trying to apply the Gestalt theory, the teacher confronts the student with the total situation bearing on the particular adapted reaction desired. The environment is so arranged as to stimulate recall of pertinent previous experience, which brings to the student a realization of the significant aspects and their basic relationships. The student is rehearsed in this situation until the various cues fuse into a meaningful pattern (a Gestalt) for him. He gets the idea, he grasps the meaning, his experience fuses into a comprehended relationship. He has learned.

The claims for whole as contrasted with part learning, the idea that the first orientation of the beginner should involve presentation by demonstration of "the general idea" or "gross-framework idea" of the skill, and the hypothesis that one develops a kinesthetic image of the skill pattern through mental rehearsal, all seem to be ramifications of the Gestalt approach to learning. Psychologists long ago demonstrated that material which could be made meaningful was much easier to learn than material demanding pure rote memorization. Retention after the same amount of practice is also much greater for meaningful material. But the point must not be overlooked that we have many types of knowledge to acquire, many responses to habituate, that are not meaningful when we first must acquire them.

PERCEPTION

Any kind of learning is the adjustment of responses to stimuli or stimulus situations. But before one can make the appropriate response, he must perceive (recognize) the stimulus. Even though these recognitions may be subliminal at times, there must be familiarity with the stimulus in order for adapted response to be made. This recognition of stimulus or stimulus situation is called "perception."

Motor learning has often been called perceptual-motor learning (see page 4 and particularly footnote 3). The word "perceptual" is introduced into the motor learning term because the stimuli need to be recognized by the subject before he can act adequately. The recognition, as well as the adapted action, has to be learned. We call your attention to the slowness of early perceptual learning described in the studies of Senden and Miner (see Chapter I, p. 5). This recognition of the stimulus or, more exactly stated, of the "stimulus pattern," makes up a great part of our learning, and seems to increase in importance as we progress up the hierarchical scale of learning complexity and maturity. We learn to recognize people, words, objects, smells, and sounds. We learn to recognize movements of others as being the beginnings of certain acts. Early in childhood we learned to recognize sensations of slight loss of balance and to respond appropriately.

Perceptions, once learned, are automatic responses to specific types of stimuli. They are the synthesis of the incoming stimuli and the associated experiential background already programmed into one's nervous system. The response may be merely a feeling of familiarity, our awareness of meaning, or even a subliminal but completely adapted motor response.

perceptual-motor patterns [10]

The individual learns perceptual-motor patterns—to run, to jump, to throw, and perhaps to swim, to skate, and to ride a bicycle. Each of these patterns involves adjustments in terms of perception. He learns speech, handwriting, all the skills of eating and dressing, and perhaps typing, dancing, or playing a musical instrument. All of these are patterns intimately tied to perception, whether visual, kinesthetic, or auditory. The learned pattern may be simple and highly integrated—the throwing act or the catching act, for example—or it may be relatively complex and persist over a period of time—the two-and-a-half off the diving board, the double play around second base in baseball, or the down-and-out-cut and reception of a forward pass in football. Most of the muscular pattern may be postural control, including much inhibitory response. Think of the inhibition of movement essential for markmanship, balancing acts, or, for that matter, any skill requiring steadiness and fineness of control. Consider also the precision in perception and the constant feedback of perceived information essential for these performances.

motor-pattern learning, especially at the higher levels, emphasizes perceptual discrimination and automatic action [11]

The youngster about to learn to throw a baseball or kick a football already has all the necessary movements and much of the postural-base control in his repertoire. He now learns a total, more complex, highly integrated continuity of action, a new pattern or a series of new patterns, to fit his new purpose. The adolescent or adult who is learning to drive a car needs to learn to perceive the cues to action, and then to select and integrate the appropriate movements. He has made, thousands of times, all the separate movements which he must now learn to integrate into his new patterns of action. His problems are: (1) perception, (2) movement selection, and (3) integration of these movements into the unit of action. He must learn *not how* but *when* to press on the accelerator or the brake pedal. He must learn the appropriate degree of force to apply as indicated by the perceived situation. Force and range of movement in turning the steering wheel are learned from the feedback of results and his continual revision in attempt to improve. Each range of movement, each force to apply, and the timing of the respective movements are adjustments learned from playback of results when reacting to perceived situations. Foot and hand movements are integrated into an automatized continuity of responses to successive cue per-

---

[10] See "Definition of Motor Learning," Chapter I, p. 4.
[11] See "Learning a New Movement *vs.* Motor Pattern Learning," Chapter I, pp. 8–9.

ception. As the skills of driving develop, they involve extensive perceptual learning and subsequent automatic action, such as the discriminative perceptions and reactions to stop signals, speed zones, variations in road width, unevenness of road surface, chance pedestrians, and congested traffic. Successful driving is impossible without continual cue reception and continual feedback of results of initiated adjustments. Much of the movement adjustment and correction becomes automatic response to arriving cues. The driver learns to integrate much of his earlier simpler learning into the complexity of these new skills.

cue reduction in perception

A cue means a stimulus from the situation which has attached to it, through learning, an association with adapted response, a feeling of familiarity, or both. Each cue is one "sub-s" ("s_1") in the total

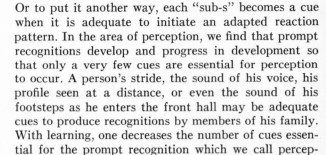

Or to put it another way, each "sub-s" becomes a cue when it is adequate to initiate an adapted reaction pattern. In the area of perception, we find that prompt recognitions develop and progress in development so that only a very few cues are essential for perception to occur. A person's stride, the sound of his voice, his profile seen at a distance, or even the sound of his footsteps as he enters the front hall may be adequate cues to produce recognitions by members of his family. With learning, one decreases the number of cues essential for the prompt recognition which we call perception. Think of any environmental situation as one in which various stimuli and various types of stimuli activate sense organs; viz.,

Any smaller number or even only one of the sub-s's can become the stimulus for prompt recognition. All our lives we learn to substitute a cue, a bit or element out of a total situation, for the original total stimulus situation, and we respond immediately without

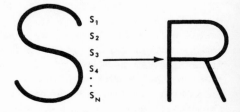

awaiting or without needing the remainder of the original total situation to produce the appropriate learned response. At times when the alarm clock clicks, I reach out to turn it off before it has time to ring, even though I am not sufficiently awake to be fully conscious of my act. The noon hour strikes and I get a hunger response although I may be in no need of food after a late breakfast. A red light suddenly appears as I drive along the avenue and my foot pushes on the brake before I have time to think about the reason. The husband barely starts a sentence and the wife breaks in to complete it for him and to add the answer.

The decrease with learning in the number of cues essential for recognition is due to the filling in of the rest of the stimulus pattern from a mental construct already established from previous experience. The term "mental construct" is merely our verbal symbolism to represent the phenomenon characteristic of highly trained perception, which produces the filling in of the whole stimulus situation from a greatly reduced number of cues. The very speed of these trained recognitions indicates their automaticity. Naval fliers in World War II learned to recognize various types of airplanes exposed on the viewing screen only one two-hundredth of a second.

STIMULUS GENERALIZATION

In general, stimuli with considerable similarity will tend to evoke the same response. This fact is a part of the problem of stimulus generalization (transfer). A somewhat generalized stimulus may be a great advantage because complete exactness of cue reproduction is not always possible; *e.g.,* variation in word pronunciations, especially in a newly learned language. Even variation in dialects of one's own language requires the same type of stimulus generalization for one to grasp meaning. Script writing varies greatly in some individuals yet we can read many handwritings and recognize their authorship. On the other hand, similarity of stimuli may cause errors in recognition if the cues are too few and the learning has not progressed far enough. Stimulus generalization permits us to transfer responses. We have enough stimulus transfer so that we can dodge or catch various thrown objects as we see them approaching us. In fact, similarity of stimuli, hence stimulus generalization, permits us to adjust to many situations in life which we have never before encountered. We use similarity of stimuli to clarify points to others or to delude them. Acting, punning, pretending, all rely on generalization of stimuli to guide the perceptions of our observers. In puns the absurdity of the double meaning comes to us from the stimulus situation. The stimulus similarity may come from similar sounds or from unusual meanings in the particular context; *e.g.,* my dog Ben had pups so I now call him Ben Hur.

The fond mother, amused at the antics of her mischievous youngster, tries to simulate cues of anger as she scolds or punishes him. Soon the child also learns to give off false cues, of pain and repentance when he feels neither. It is often a question of who is fooling whom. The feints and fakes of sports contests are other examples of attempts to fool others through the principle of stimulus generalization. The great base runners in baseball and the great defensive men in team games need very few cues to release appropriate action; but they also have learned great discrimination between cues so as to decrease the number of errors from stimulus similarity.

Another way to look at the principle of generalization of similar stimuli might be to say that the person who generalizes is actually reacting to identical elements in the similar situations (Thorndikian theory). When I try to fake a defensive man in basketball by a head and foot movement to one side, I do make a preliminary part of the movement pattern for the drive past that side of the opponent—the head and shoulder, and perhaps foot, do start a movement in the fake direction. These false cues are taken from the total pattern of the actual act of driving by on that side. I merely cut off the act after slight preliminary moves, and drive to the other side. There will of necessity be slight differences in the center of gravity of my body when the drive is inhibited for quick reversal so early. If these slight differences in my center of gravity with relation to my base are apparent to the skilled opponent, he uses them as his cues, instead of my fakes, to initiate his acts to defeat my purpose. He has had enough experience or training to be highly discriminative in responses to cues from opponents' actions.

Learning is a complex affair and has many aspects. It involves involuntary conditioning, such as modification of pupillary response or fear of snakes. It involves the type of learning described as individuation of movements in the preceding chapter, as well as innumerable types of motor-skill accuracy acquirements. It involves many associative bonds; *e.g.*, learning names of states, capitals, presidents; conjugations and declensions; names of bones and muscles. It involves comprehension of meaning: *e.g.*, one's concept of almost any noun.

THE DEGREE OF MEANINGFULNESS

Perhaps it is a sound principle of teaching to try to classify the learning problem as to its degree of meaningfulness for the particular learner. Human maze learning, learning to hit the proper keys on the piano or typewriter keyboard, learning one's way across a strange city on foot, even the learning of some of the traditional "coordination exercises" in physical education, all involve learning a kind of serial association without much background of meaningful experience which will transfer and help to strengthen the associative links which must be formed.

Both in school and in life we have to learn many responses which are made a specific way by custom, tradition, or reasons beyond our comprehension. Spelling, multiplication tables, many dates and facts, number of days in each month are examples of this type of learning. The course in anatomy requires much memorization of names. Language study requires memorization of vocabulary, conjugations, and declensions. Remember how long you had to struggle over those foreign-language irregular verbs! Some such learning is essential in most areas of schoolwork. The student learns because he wants to succeed in school, to please his parents, to equal or surpass his classmates, and so on. Intrinsic motivation, actual interest in the content itself, is very difficult to achieve in such learning. The best the teacher can do is to convince the student that the learning is essential knowledge in the social milieu of which he will be a part, or that it is a prerequisite for some future goal he has in mind. In the learning of the so-called "coordination exercises" mentioned above, the student learns a serial sequence different for each arm but occurring simultaneously, with perhaps some additional head and trunk movements to add to the complexity, increase the difficulty, and multiply the number of unlike movements to be carried on simultaneously by various body parts. The student practices the exercise, not because he sees any use for such activity, but in order to secure teacher approval and a passing grade; or perhaps because he docilely accepts the teacher's dictum that the activity is a "worthwhile developmental exercise."

The methods used in nonmeaningful associative learning are quite different from those used with meaningful material. They involve much repetition, immediate substitution of correct response for any error, and extrinsic motivation. Recall involves speed, accuracy, rote memory; but even in rote memory learning, the learner will try to invent some sort of meaningful association, some system of like sounds or of extraneous verbal symbols, to hasten his learning. He must have some means of tying together the material into the desired sequential order.

An accompanying meaningful vocabulary tends to develop with one's skills; *i.e.*, one grows in ability to think about the activity in words. He learns to use meaningfully such words as force, speed, accuracy, balance, arc of the swing, reaction and movement time; also the names of particular activity patterns such as kip, giant swing, two-and-a-half off the diving board, or hook shot off the pivot. The nouns one uses in his thinking and communicating, whether in physical-activity areas or in academic areas, are called concepts.

THE CONCEPT

The very nature of a concept illustrates the extent to which human experience can be abstracted, synthesized, epitomized, and then reduced to the shorthand of verbal symbols without losing the lessons from the great experiential background. Perhaps a short discussion of the nature of the concept will clarify our meaning.

A concept represents a lot of experience fused into a core of meaning. It is usually an aura of meaning represented by some symbol. Words such as "dog," "car," "movie," and "ball game" are symbols which represent significant aspects of much past experience in that particular area. We do not need to recall all the specific experiences to use the concept. In fact, we probably cannot recall all the previous experience which added to our meaning of the concept. How many types of dogs passed through your realm of experience to give you your present concept of dog? Perhaps they ranged from the chihuahua to the greyhound and from the registered champions to the dozens of lost, wandering crossbred and mismated strays. The reader's concept of a "pivot" has probably developed from a background of experience in the hip rotation and shift of weight in golf, the reversal of direction in tennis, the offensive maneuver around one's man in basketball, or the innumerable turns and changes in center of gravity in the dance.

GENERALIZATIONS

Moving farther along in the continuity of meaning, we come to generalizations. They are relationships of broad applicability between two or more concepts. We have a concept of speed of movement and a concept of force of impact. We generalize that, other things being equal, the force of impact is proportional to the speed of movement. If we swing the bat or racket faster, we hit the ball harder. If we increase the speed of our body before blocking the opponent, we can hit him more forcefully. Or, in other conditions, if we cannot avoid an undesirable collision completely, we can decrease its seriousness by decreasing our speed as much as possible. This principle applies to bumping into another pedestrian or backing into another car when parking our own. The concepts of speed and force are here joined into a statement of relationship, a generalization.

SUMMARY

The individual is a unified organism and learning involves his entire being. In various degrees any learning situation tends to involve attitudes, emotions, ideas, concepts and generalizations, motor and verbal responses, implicit or overt. A drive or purpose seems to be basic to learning. Learning varies in nature and complexity from classical conditioning to highly rational and meaningful adult learning, and from simple movements to highly complex and integrated movement patterns involving various body-part individuations in a patterned sequence. There is some evidence of latent learning—occurrence of learning without apparent intent, and with no associated primary need reduction. Common classifications of learning are conditioning, associative learning (trial and error), and insight (gestalt) learning. Perhaps these are just variations in aspects of learning along a continuum.

Any kind of learning is the adjustment of responses to stimuli or stimulus situations, but before one can make an appropriate response he must learn to recognize the stimulus. Some of the stimulus recognitions are subliminal, but even with these there must be familiarity with the stimulus in order for adapted response to be made. This recognition of stimulus at whatever level of consciousness is called perception.

Motor-pattern (skill) learning involves perception of stimulus situation, movement selection, and integration of the selected movements into a unit of action. Much of the movement selection and integration is brought about by adjustment from feedback of results by proprioceptive facilitation. As learning progresses, fewer cues from the stimulus situation are needed to release an adapted response. Moreover, the speed of the cue recognition is greatly increased.

Stimulus generalization develops so that similar stimuli evoke like responses. Man gradually develops symbols to represent great areas of experience. The symbol stands for a concept—a wealth of experience abstracted, synthesized, epitomized into an aura of meaning and tied to appropriately adapted responses. Generalizations are relationships between concepts.

A background of selected, organized, and interpreted experience (meaning) carries with it many strong associative links. When the material to be learned can be made meaningful in this sense, it is easier to learn, is retained longer, and is much more likely to transfer to new situations. Meaningful material already possesses transferred relationships from previous learning and can be further linked to one's experiences by instructor stimulus of recall of additional past applicable experience and guidance in present applications. When the advanced-skill learner sees the purpose or object of the new skill, he makes many meaningful adaptations from his previous experience. When the material to be learned is lacking in meaning (not clarified by past experience), it must be learned through drill, rote memory, and extrinsic motivation.

discussion questions

1. May one learn without being aware that he is learning?
2. Are mental, physical, and emotional adjustments through experience completely different and isolated types of learning?
3. Are complacency and satisfaction conducive to learning?
4. Do the different categories of learning merely indicate degree of emphasis on certain aspects of the learning; *i.e.,* is there a continuity of the learning processes from simplest to highest types of learning?
5. May one be learning in situations in which he has no intention or desire to learn?
6. Does unconscious and involuntary response conditioning occur in the well-educated, normal adult?
7. Are children occasionally conditioned by parents in certain attitudes and reactions without the parents' intent or awareness of so doing?
8. May "trial-and-error" learning occur without overt expression of the trials?
9. Is the occasional effectiveness of "punishment" in facilitating learning due to the feedback of information of results of action; *i.e.,* clarification of more effective response?
10. Is the "sudden emergence of a complete solution" (Gestalt learning as described by Köhler) the typical way that motor-skill learning occurs?
11. Is "insight" merely highly sophisticated mental trial and error?
12. Does the incubation stage in creative imagination imply the occurrence of a reorganization of the background of information carried on below the level of conscious awareness?
13. Do any of the theories of learning in this chapter encompass the cybernetic hypothesis (electronic computer, servomechanisms, and constant feedback) as to human adaptation and adjustment hypothesized in Chapter I? *
14. Are the most suitable teaching procedures for meaningful and nonmeaningful material the same?
15. Is perceptual learning a basic and increasingly important factor in the development of high motor-skill levels?

DEFINE:

Cue

Stimulus generalization

Concept

Generalization

---

* Consult also K. U. Smith and M. F. Smith, *Cybernetic Principles of Learning and Educational Design* (New York: Holt, Rinehart, and Winston, Inc., 1966).

IV

Methods in
Early Stages
of Skill Learning

IMITATION; MOVEMENT ADJUSTMENTS BELOW
THE LEVEL OF CONSCIOUS AWARENESS

Before beginning the discussion of methods, certain facts
about procedures in motor learning should be mentioned. For
example, at times even a child seems to be able, merely from
observing an adult engaged in relatively simple activities, to
imitate him in what resembles, at least in gross pattern, the
action of the adult. Many acts are performed somewhat effectively and rather promptly by imitation after direct observation. In this connection we should mention a principle long
established by physiologists—namely, that movements, not
muscles, are represented in the cortex; in other words, supra-
threshold stimulus of the cortex releases more or less integrated
movement patterns. Moreover, a muscle itself may be stimulated from various parts of the cortex.

Next we should mention that many highly skilled individuals
are unaware of exactly how they perform particular skills.
Much of the learning of skilled behavior goes on beneath the
level of conscious awareness. Let me quote a few psychologists
on this point. In 1927 Bowdlear, in summarizing one of his
studies, said:

> Man would be at a decided disadvantage if he could not
> learn by trial and error since often the thing he has to manage
> is very difficult to learn through rational analysis. Much motor
> skill is acquired by doing the best you can; getting into
> trouble, varying your procedure, and gradually "getting the
> hang of the thing" without ever clearly seeing what are the con-
> ditions of success.[1]

---

[1] Charles W. Bowdlear, "An Experiment in Kinesthetic Learning,"
American Physical Education Review, XXXII:2 (February 1927), 100.

Bartlett stated this more succinctly when speaking about the muscular part of a skilled operation: "The more efficient it is, the less is known about it." [2] U. T. Place, a British psychologist states the same idea as follows:

> Close attention to his own activity will be of no avail to the unskilled person because he has not learnt to discriminate between the relevant and the irrelevant features. . . . On the other hand an acute consciousness of the details of his own activity in relation to the environment may actually detract from the efficiency of performance in the case of an individual who has learnt to make many of the adjustments involved automatically. Thus we say frequently of someone whose skill is already well developed that his performance suffered because he paid too close attention to what he was doing. [3]

Bartlett comments on the fact that key cues only rise to awareness in the execution of certain skills; that the bulk of what is happening proceeds at levels below consciousness. [4]

The assumption made here is that there are various levels of consciousness, from the focus of attention (used herein to imply the awareness level) on down to the unconscious. The latter implies content which cannot normally be brought to the awareness level; *i.e.*, to conscious attention. For example, varying levels of consciousness are active when one is driving a car while talking to a companion and, at the same time, considering other matters not covered by the social conversation. He adjusts the brake or the accelerator and rotates the steering wheel appropriately to incoming cues. The actions are largely automatic and only the stronger cues from the highway cause complete focus of his attention. Of course, if he drives with too great inattention, he becomes a hazardous driver. The way in which one directs his attention (or perhaps at times the way in which his attention is directed by interest, strength of competing stimuli, etc.) affects the vividness of his consciousness, the difference in clearness of objects and of the various other factors in the environmental situation.

The writer recalls two instances which may be helpful in illustrating the pattern-nature and the fact that the performer has only a gross-outline-awareness of much motor behavior. While a graduate student at Columbia over a generation ago, when it was still safe to walk alone at night through the poorer parts of the city, he used to take a subway down to Chatham Square and walk across town to Greenwich Village. This stroll was a post-midnight means of relaxing after several hours of study. One night while browsing through Pell and Mott Streets, he noted a poor crippled hunchback lurching along with a very irregular hitch and limp in his peculiar locomotion. Four street urchins playing in the street at this late hour, perhaps because it was too hot to go to bed or because they had no responsible parents to guide them, paused in their play and observed the cripple, apparently with some interest. Then as he passed them, they fell in behind in a line, imitating

---

[2] Frederick C. Bartlett, "The Measurement of Human Skill," *British Medical Journal* (June 21, 1947), p. 877.

[3] U. T. Place, "The Concept of Heed," *British Journal of Psychology*, XLV (November 1954), 247.

[4] Bartlett, *op. cit.*

his lurching, hitching stride so well that an observer could not help recognizing the close resemblance. They seemed to be a family group of queer creatures, all with the same grotesque means of locomotion. A hundred feet down the block, the urchins dropped off and returned to their former play and the cripple was now apparently out of mind as well as out of sight.

Some years later the writer was reclining not far from the first tee at a country club golf course. Four men of very mediocre golfing ability, and with quite varied builds and stature, stepped up to the tee and took their first drives. Each had his peculiar stance and form, affected perhaps by too much time at the table or by too frequent playing of the "nineteenth hole." After they had gone on down the course, one of the caddies who had been waiting for jobs back in the shade of a nearby tree stepped up to the tee and proceeded to give his fellow caddies such a close imitation of the drives of the preceding men that no one who had observed would have failed to identify each one being imitated. True, there was a bit of exaggeration of the varied mannerisms, but only enough to etch out more clearly the one being imitated.

It seems likely in each of the above cases that the imitations were improvisations of the moment, previously unpracticed. The gross-pattern imitation illustrates the way a human body may respond in unified movement patterns to what is merely a retained general idea of an observed action.

HOW SHOULD WE START THE BEGINNER?
THE GROSS-FRAMEWORK IDEA

In motor-skill learning the best results seem to be obtained when the learner's first attempts are endeavors to grasp and respond to the unit idea, the general idea, the gross-framework idea of the pattern which represents his purpose. He seems to learn more readily during motivated practice if he delegates the major part of the movement adjustment, the filling in of the gross framework, to lower levels of consciousness. His attention is not directed to the details of the movements but rather to the general-impression memory of the gross outline of the skill. In other words, conscious awareness should not attend to the movements which make up the act, but should focus on the desired results of the movements and allow the lower levels of attention to control the movements. This imitative behavior, this activity in which the novice attempts to approximate the gross act, seems to be possible, at least to some degree, as soon as the individual has acquired the primary sensory-motor adaptations of infant and nursery school development. It is not uncommon to see the four-year-old attempt imitations of what seems to be a gross-framework idea of the behavior of the adult he is imitating.

The term "general idea" or "gross-framework idea" does not imply a generalization from a number of preceding experiences; rather it implies a possibly vague outline impression, but a memory of some sort of a preceding demonstration or observed performance. This outline impression guides the learner in his attempts, and is not reflected in a smooth or polished performance; at first it usually results in just a crude approximation of that which he is trying to learn. Smooth and polished performance must await specific, motivated practice with performance being gradually adjusted from feedback of results.

This "general idea" of the action-pattern might be strengthened by some attention to some "etched" positions (not movements) in the pattern. These positions can serve as checkpoints for both presentation and performance. The gross idea of the initial or preparatory position for the act, then, of the arc and direction of the movement and of the final position in the act might be sequentially imaged in a panoramic flow of the gross-framework idea through consciousness. In throwing, batting, stroking with a racket, and the like, etched positions might be (1) the side stance with the leverage arm (the one which holds the implement or ball) to the rear, (2) a general impression of the path of this acting arm as it moves, and (3) the swing through with the other side of the body taking the forward position. You can make your own "gross framework" for teaching a child to kick a football —catch or grasp it, set, drop it, and kick. These phases are aspects which should stand out as his attention diffuses over the whole act and moves ahead to the next aspect while he is performing the preceding.

HOW SHOULD THE TEACHER IMPART
THE GROSS-FRAMEWORK IDEA?

The method of giving the beginner this "general idea" of the skill varies with the teacher and with the student. Demonstration has tended to be the most successful method for the more apt learner and has been shown to be successful for the average learner also, if the skill is not too complex for his level of development. It is perhaps the best, quick guess of what should be tried out first with all groups. However, demonstration by itself is unlikely to be completely adequate with special groups such as low-skill learners, the very young, or the very old.

When working with the special groups just mentioned, the skills usually need to be introduced in very simple units. Manual manipulation, to assist the efforts of the subject in his early attempts to perform the skill, will often serve as an effective supplement or even as a substitute for demonstration in "etching" the gross pattern in the minds of these special cases. Verbal explanation and description by the teacher appears to be the most commonly used method of imparting the general idea, but its value appears to have been greatly exaggerated and its use generally overstressed.

verbal guidance

Some experimental studies might help to clarify this point. Rivenes experimented with the learning of golf putting and of soccer kicking by complete novices. He used college students as subjects so that inadequate general vocabulary would be less likely to be a factor influencing the effectiveness of verbal presentations. He simplified his vocabulary so that it seemed to include only words which were already in the current vocabulary of the subjects.

Rivenes' control group was given demonstrations for the first four to five minutes of the first six practices, but no verbal guidance. His experimental group had exactly the same demonstrations, plus two to three minutes of carefully worked out verbal explanation and description which accompanied the demonstration at each of the first six practices. The assumption was made that the two to three minutes of extra time for the verbal explanation given during the first six days of the experimental group's practice would not increase the total learning time significantly. Rivenes measured learning rate, and retention after eight weeks without practice, for both the verbal and nonverbal groups. The only significant difference between the two groups in either learning or retention was in scores on a verbal written test in which the subjects tried to furnish verbal answers describing form and performance of the skill. The actual mean scores on physical performance, either in learning or in retention after eight weeks without practice, were not significantly different. Mean time to learn to the criterion was slightly less for the nonverbal group and their scores were higher for retention, but the difference was so small as to be almost surely just chance fluctuation.

Rivenes did find quite a significant correlation between scores on the verbal test and the rate of learning of the verbal-instruction group, but no such correlation for the nonverbal group. The fact that the scores of the two groups were not different in learning rate or retention indicates that the verbal group used a somewhat different, although not more efficient, learning procedure.[5]

form

One problem which the teacher must answer before trying to present to the learner the gross-framework idea of the skill has to do with form. Form is "the way to do it," the work method, the design of performance. In general, the teacher should use some form which has proved highly successful for past performers. Of course, a real problem arises here in the more complex skills because the experts tend to be characterized by a diversity rather than uniformity of forms.

Generally speaking, the teacher should use some relatively simple form with the beginner, but yet one which employs sound mechanics and which is, if possible, somewhat adapted to the functional and structural characteristics of the specific learner. Fortunately the learner will tend to adapt a gross-framework pattern to his own abilities by making adjustments in terms of ease and success. In fact, the focus on gross outline in imparting the general idea of the skill, instead of attention to precise detail, has the advantage of this greater probability of adaptation to the individual's structural and functional characteristics. Moreover, many demonstrations involve details

[5] Richard Sven Rivenes, "Effect on Motor Skill Acquisition and Retention of Teaching by Demonstration With and Without Verbal Explanation" (unpublished Master's thesis, The Pennsylvania State University, 1961).

and mannerisms peculiar to the specific demonstrator, and perhaps related to mediocre performance by the demonstrator. If the learner gets the general idea and is motivated to practice, he will gradually adjust his performance to his own individuality as a result of his feedback of practice results. In other words, his desire for most effective achievement of his purpose or goal causes a revision of his responses following feedback of each performance-result.

Once the beginner has the general idea and starts to practice, he will make many adjustments without consciousness of the precise movement selection made. Minor errors are unimportant at this stage because movements change as speeds change or as skill advances; and minor errors will tend to drop out. The polish of parts should be left to the advanced stages when the student will tend to fill in mentally the rest of the unit pattern. Only at this advanced stage does part-practice have real meaning. At this stage the part becomes an overtly expressed bit of a mentally conceived whole.

attention is not on movement

To begin to understand this idea that much movement selection and integration go on below the level of conscious awareness, let us consider a few experimental approaches to teaching.

In 1931 Coleman Griffith blindfolded a group of beginning golfers for their first four weeks of a six-week session. He compared them with a similar group who took their early lessons in the normal manner and reported that the ones who had begun their learning with sessions in which they were blindfolded were superior at the end.[6]

Frazier taught one group of beginners to serve a tennis ball in a completely dark indoor court, for the first three-fourths of their experimental sessions, then brought them out to a regular court in daylight for the final sessions. The orientation these learners had received for their training in the dark area was a view of a brilliantly lighted loop film of the tennis serve. The balls were luminous, and the footline, net line, and the racket frame were painted with luminous paint. She reported very slightly superior learning in her experimental group as compared to a control group taught outside in the daylight.[7]

Hoyt Sherman devised a method which accelerated the rate of learning of his beginning drawing classes at Ohio State University to such an extent that they learned in less than half the time required by groups taught by traditional methods. His experimental groups were placed in a completely dark room and each subject was placed at a desk on which were a large set of canvasses and adequate charcoal. The subjects were then given a $\frac{1}{10}$-second exposure of a well lighted picture which they were to draw. Following each exposure, they were again in complete darkness and were given one

---

[6] Coleman R. Griffith, "An Experiment on Learning to Drive a Golf Ball," *The Athletic Journal*, XI:10 (June 1931), 11–13.

[7] Vivian Frazier, "The Effects of Visual Limitations on the Rate of Learning of the Tennis Serve" (unpublished Master's thesis, The Pennsylvania State College, 1952).

minute to sketch the figure they had just seen. Each day Sherman gave them twenty different figures to draw and twenty minutes (one minute per drawing) to sketch. He explained the success of this method of teaching by saying that he taught them to see by perceptual unity.[8]

In 1947 Berlin completed a study of the learning of a fine motor skill under what she called conditions of diffused attention. The skill was practiced by her various groups under the influence of different variables. The control group just practiced the skill. A second group was required to listen to various musical selections while practicing the skill. A third group had a series of additional activities to carry on simultaneously while practicing the skill. These extra activities included adding columns of numbers, reading a story, cancelling misspelled words in a poem, and counting dots. After a considerable span of learning time, Berlin reversed the environmental and "distracting" situations of the second and third groups for a further series of lessons.

Berlin concluded:

> Diffusing the learner's attention during the process of learning a fine motor skill, after the orientation period is completed, is conducive to greater learning.[9]

In 1958 Cugini decided that Berlin's findings must surely be due to some error in experimental procedure. On the basis of this hypothesis, Cugini undertook an experiment which was quite similar in design to Berlin's. However, Cugini changed the skill to three-ball juggling and increased the degree of "distraction." Her subjects recited the alphabet backward, spelled words backward, and solved arithmetic problems in addition, subtraction, multiplication, and division while they were practicing juggling. Moreover, Cugini increased the difficulty of the mental problems to be solved as the experiment progressed. She rotated the groups so that Group I had distractions during the first and third weeks, but Group II had distractions only during the second week. In spite of her emphasis on the distractions, she was not able to obtain faster learning by her nondistracted group. She concluded that the distraction made no significant difference in the rate of learning.[10]

The studies of Berlin and Cugini are not completely comparable. Berlin used a fine motor skill and Cugini used a gross motor skill; moreover, Cugini increased the difficulty of the distracting task progressively as the experiment continued. Perhaps the most important difference is that Berlin based her conclusions on 160 minutes of spaced practice whereas Cugini based her conclusions on only seventy-two minutes of spaced practice.

---

[8] Hoyt L. Sherman *et al., Drawing by Seeing* (New York: Hinds, Hayden & Eldredge, Inc., 1947).

[9] Pearl Berlin, "An Experimental Study of the Learning of a Fine Motor Skill under Conditions of Diffused Attention" (unpublished Master's thesis, The Pennsylvania State University, 1947), p. 182.

[10] Elizabeth D. Cugini, "The Effect on Gross Motor Skill Attainment of Varying the Degree of Attention Focus During the Learning Process" (unpublished Master's thesis, The Pennsylvania State University, 1959).

In those studies just cited in which early practices were conducted in the dark, with blindfolds on the learners, or under so-called distracting conditions, we find a clue to the most effective direction of attention during the early stages of motor learning. Griffith thought that his procedure directed attention toward "feel" or kinesthetic perception; Sherman thought his procedure forced one to learn by "perceptual unity"—to see the whole image as a unit. Frazier did not try a hypothetical explanation. The "distraction" studies of Berlin and Cugini seem to have been designed so as to keep the focus of attention of the learner *off the movements* although the general idea of the act remained at least in the periphery of consciousness and probably came into focus momentarily with great frequency. Apparently attention should be directed *away from the movements* and *toward the general idea* in the early stages of motor learning.

Two hypotheses have been suggested as reasons for the favorable effects of "inattention" on performance; namely, (1) by attending to a muscular act, one is probably inhibiting the action of subliminal cues that are necessary for the integrations and adjustments in the act, and (2) consciousness cannot act on the basis of past experience that is, in itself, unconscious.[11]

Hellebrandt, after discussing the great importance of the proprioceptive system, says:

> Feedback from the muscles, tendons and joints appears to be a cunningly devised and exceedingly complex mechanism, a large share of which operates at levels below consciousness. Not only has automation come to industry. We now know that the machinery of the living body is equipped with its own servo-mechanisms. Its operation proceeds to a large extent without placing the slightest demand on the cerebral cortex. Innumerable mechanisms exist which are beyond the reach of the most astute physical therapist or teacher of physical education. Perhaps what we need most are techniques of motor learning that free the subcortical motor mechanisms from an oppressive domination of a stressed cortex. Starting from scratch, decorticated as it were, primitively integrated, we might then explore the wonders of that inherent, ancestral movement repertoire and use it as nature intended before encephalization produced its present degree of tension and inhibition.[12]

Hellebrandt's point about the great importance of proprioception in motor learning should not be divorced from her statement that its operation tends to occur below the level of conscious awareness. "Kinesthesis," "the feel of the movement," "a conscious muscle sense" are terms that have all been used extensively in the literature, many times with the apparent assumption that such "sensing" in skill adjustment was a conscious, rationally directed type of learning. Experimental evidence does not support this viewpoint although it does indicate great value to proprioceptive sensing and adjustment.

---

[11] Consult James Grier Miller, *Unconsciousness* (New York: John Wiley and Sons, Inc., 1942), Chap. VI, "Subliminal Unconsciousness."

[12] Frances A. Hellebrandt, *Physiology of Motor Learning* (her condensation from a Seminar presented at the University of Wisconsin on January 21, 1958, while serving as Visiting Lecturer in the Department of Physical Education for Women). See *Cerebral Palsy Review*, XIX:4 (July-August 1958), p. 11.

does the direction of attention
change as skill increases?

Gallagher decided to study further this problem of direction of attention. He designed an experiment in which he taught three-ball juggling to beginners and took high-speed movies of their visual behavior during the various stages of the learning. His assumption was that the visual focus would be a fairly good index of the direction of attention. He also compared the visual behavior of those of high skill level with those of low skill level. Gallagher found that, as learning advanced, the subjects came more and more to a standard behavior of using a "distant stare" directed through the peak of the parabola of the path of the three juggled balls. The advanced-skill-level subjects had reduced vertical eye movements to zero and horizontal eye movements to nearly zero. Gallagher hypothesized that the acquisition of the skill depended on this direction of attention to such visual cues to movement as were received from far distant focus, relatively still eyes, and stimuli passing through the visual periphery.[13]

SHOULD WE FORCE HYPOTHETICALLY
CORRECT BEHAVIOR ON THE NOVICE?

Another student followed up Gallagher's study and investigated the problem of whether or not forcing the novice from the beginning of practice to use this hypothetically correct visual behavior would accelerate her rate of learning. (I say "her" because Miss Bush used only female subjects.)

Bush's study produced some interesting data which we are still puzzling over. She used only twenty novice subjects in her experimental group and twenty in her control group. They were equated on a one-ball "juggling-coordination test" which had been previously validated.

At all practices during the experiment her experimental group wore "blinders" which prevented vision below the horizontal level of the eye. The blinders were merely opaque material attached to the lower arc of glasses frames and fitted neatly beneath each eye. Both the frames and material were very light in weight, hence not annoying because of pressure on the subject. Her control group underwent exactly the same practice regimens except that they had no artificial factor to force them into the hypothetically successful visual behavior; in other words, no "blinders." Both groups were started with two or three demonstrations of the juggling and a few verbal suggestions, but they had no further instruction during the succeeding practices.

Bush found no significant difference in the learning of her six best subjects in the respective groups. She says that the six fast learners in her control group quickly adopted the same pattern that the six fast learners in her

---

[13] James Dennis Gallagher, "A Study of Eye Movements and Visual Focus During the Learning of Juggling" (unpublished Master's thesis, The Pennsylvania State University, 1961).

experimental group were being forced to use. There were five or six at the bottom of the experimental group who, during the whole course of the experiment, did not learn to toss three balls in any juggling pattern so that they could make more than two to seven successive catches. Bush hypothesized about this group that she had started them with too complex a unit (three-ball juggling) for their present level of motor-learning development.

The startling thing about her experiment was that no one of the remaining fourteen of her control group did any better than the poorest six in the experimental group. Although the experiment must be repeated, the number of subjects increased, and the total practice time lengthened before the conclusions can be more than hypotheses, Bush concluded somewhat as follows: (1) the apt students in a particular skill need little beyond the general idea of what the skill is, a desire to learn, and the opportunity to practice; (2) the very inept do not seem to learn much in spite of additional help; (3) the average student can progress rather steadily if she is provided with enough guidance and restriction to make the practice performances become attempts to approximate, at least grossly, the major aspects of the successful pattern.[14]

SHOULD WE LET THE LEARNER MAKE ERRORS?

Dr. John E. Anderson has said:

> It is clear that errors are significant parts of the process of organizing a skill. In some degree the individual must be permitted to make his own errors in order that the learning process may go forward.[15]

You might think a moment about this statement, and then consider the experiment in which Bush forced her novice subjects into the visual behavior which they would use if they became proficient in the skill. It is a generally accepted principle that replacement of a less efficient performance-habit by a more effective one is much more difficult after erroneous performance has persisted some time. However, we do learn from our errors. It is from the feedback of results that we learn to avoid errors and adjust. Dr. Pearl Berlin, commenting in a lecture on the need for experience of error in order to discriminate the effective from the ineffective, said: "For example, one has to fall down to learn to ski but he does not have to break a leg."

Perhaps we might hypothesize that failure to correct *major* errors early, for the average or slow learner, would retard the learning. The teacher should be alert to step in and correct a major error if it seems to be persisting after several trials. Violation of known principles of mechanics, such as using

[14] Jone J. Bush, "The Effect of Motor Learning of Forcing Hypothetically Correct Visual Behavior on the Learner" (unpublished Master's thesis, The Pennsylvania State University, 1961).

[15] John E. Anderson, "Growth and Development Today: Implications for Physical Education (Paper presented at National Conference on Social Changes and Implications for Physical Education and Sports Recreation, Estes Park, Colorado, June 1958).

only the arm or not flexing the knees or trunk when throwing for distance or speed, are major errors because they deviate from the gross framework of the skill. The teacher should not, at this stage, correct supposed errors which do not deviate markedly from the gross pattern.

correction of persisting errors

As the skill advances toward higher levels, the problem of persisting error arises. Such error is usually some variation in form which violates some basic mechanical principle, but which is repeated until it begins to be a part of the automatized performance. The learner does not know what he is doing inefficiently, so he fails to adjust performance from the feedback of results. He continues the same inefficient aspect, tries harder to succeed, but merely thrusts the error deeper into the unconsciousness of automaticity. He begins to develop cover-up, compensatory adjustments which produce low-level successes but which handicap him for higher-level performance.

The tennis player who runs around his backhand, the baseball player who fails to shift his weight behind his throw and throws almost entirely with his arm, the hurdler who jumps over the hurdles, or the basketball player who always dribbles with a preferred hand (one side only) are examples of this problem. The error may be harder to analyze: *e.g.*, one involving a preparatory postural base with inadequate limb flexion, or disadvantageous position of the body's center of gravity over its base. It may be a line of movement of the elbow which does not permit the most powerful push in shot putting; or, in team games, habitual ball transfer to teammates in such a way as to retard their subsequent actions. It may be such a simple error as not putting the receiving hand at right angles to line of flight of the ball in the catching act; *i.e.*, trying instead to trap the ball between two hands extended parallel to the ball line of flight.

The teacher will need to bring the error to the conscious attention of the learner. Perhaps the teacher will need to demonstrate in slow motion the erroneous performance, then have the learner repeat it until he brings that part of the action to the awareness level of consciousness. Then the substitute part may be introduced into the total act. Once incorporated into the total pattern, the correction must then be practiced until it becomes a part of a new automatic performance.

RELATIVE EFFECTIVENESS OF FIVE METHODS

Berlin studied the effect of five different teaching methods on the rate of acquisition of a specific skill in golf, soccer, fencing, tennis, and lacrosse. She used a total of 111 college women divided into five groups. They were all given a general orientation to the five skills, then were taught the five skills one at a time, with different instruction methods for each skill. The methods used after the general orientation were: (1) demonstration plus practice, (2) trial-and-error practice only, (3) verbal instruction plus practice, (4) visual aids plus practice, and (5) a combination of the preceding four. The learning time for the trial-and-error group was entirely devoted to practice.

In the other groups, some time was used for the demonstrating, explaining, or showing of movies. Berlin designed her experiment so that each method was tried out on each skill but with a different group as the method changed. Each group experienced all five methods; *i.e.*, golf was taught to Group I by demonstration and practice, to Group II by trial and error only, to Group III by verbal detail and practice, to Group IV by visual aids and practice, and to Group V by a combination of these methods. Then she compared the time it took each group to learn a skill under the respective methods, and ranked the methods as to effectiveness for most rapid learning per skill and for the five skills. The trial-and-error method proved to be the most efficient, and the combination of methods ranked second.[16] Berlin commented with respect to the verbal-instruction method as follows:

> Words have little meaning for the beginner in motor skills (such as these). It appears that the need for verbalization by the teacher is increased somewhat proportionately with the learner's increased experience in performing the skill. An adult learner may ask for verbal direction; an instructor might do well not to interfere with the learning process until such questions are raised or until interruption is deemed absolutely necessary.[17]

Several other studies have reported little value to verbal explanation as a means of giving the beginner the general idea of what he is to practice. It seems that the most effective methods are: show him the act, then let him try it out; demonstrate again if necessary; point out major aspects; guide him manually if necessary; and let him practice.

METHODS WITH EXCEPTIONAL SUBJECTS

Dailey studied the methods of teaching motor skills to the sensory handicapped (the deaf, the blind, and the deaf-blind), and then compared these methods with methods used to teach (1) very young children; (2) senior citizens; and (3) low-skilled students at various educational levels. Except for skills which place great emphasis on balance, she found no retardation of motor skill learning due to deafness. Manual manipulation by the teacher, and having the learner feel the movements of the demonstrator, tended to be the best methods to give the blind the "general idea" of what to practice. To be effective, the manual manipulation must be a guiding, with the learner trying to move as guided. It must not be a passive, unconcerned submission to having one's limbs moved as the teacher wills.[18]

---

[16] Note that each group was given a "general idea" or "gross-framework-idea" of the skill in the orientation which preceded the introduction of the five method-variables. Note also that the skills she used were basic and highly integrated skills chosen from each sport.

[17] Pearl Berlin, "Effects of Varied Teaching Emphases During Early Learning on Acquisition of Selected Motor Skills" (unpublished doctoral thesis, The Pennsylvania State University, 1959), p. 196.

[18] Jacqueline Dailey, "Methods in Motor Learning as Revealed Through a Study of the Sensory Handicapped" (unpublished Master's thesis, The Pennsylvania State University, 1961).

From what few data we have been able to gather so far, it is apparent that demonstration often needs the supplement of mechanical manipulation with infants or primary school children, and with low-skill-level students at any age, when they are trying to learn what seem to them to be complex skills. We have checked procedures among teachers who have had much experience with the teaching of very young children—for example, with Turner instructors who often start the children at gymnastics, and particularly tumbling, at the age of two or three—and have found wide use of manual manipulation but very little use of verbal description. As to advanced age, Berlin has made extensive use of manipulation in getting senior-citizen beginners oriented in their first lessons in swimming. Her subjects were in the sixth, seventh, and eighth decades of their lives.[19] Incidentally, she had great success in teaching them to swim.[20]

VALUE OF VERBAL TEACHING VARIES
WITH NATURE OF SUBJECT AND SKILL

When the skill is made up of a number of units which the learner has already performed, perhaps of movement patterns which are already tied to verbal symbols, then verbal explanation is more successful and may be the quickest way to teach the skill. This is particularly so, it seems, if pictures or demonstrations of each act accompany the verbal description. Many motor tasks, even the army rifle assemblage, can be taught to large numbers of people more economically this way. The value of verbal explanation increases in many complex skills as the learner gets beyond the novice stage. The words now may have meaning in terms of past acts and their results—acts which may have become partially verbalized by the learner as he has tied them into the gross pattern of his present skill.

In trying to evaluate the importance of verbal instruction in motor learning, one must take into account the nature of the skill, the nature of the specific learner, and the nature and purpose of the verbal instruction. Some skills are very difficult to describe verbally, hence directions as to how to perform them are lacking in meaning; for example, pursuit-rotor skills and skills involving varying types of balance do not seem to lend themselves to verbal explanation as to "how to do." Moreover, some learners are better able to understand and follow verbal directions than are others. The vocabulary used to describe the skill may have little meaning for young children, for low-skilled persons, and even for the complete beginner in the particular skill. This latter point is what Sir W. G. Stimpson had in mind when he said, concerning the first lessons in golf:

---

[19] Here again it should be noted that the sixty- to eighty-year-olds wore ear plugs as a health factor; and in the water without their glasses, many could see none too well. These limiting factors seem to have required the use of the manual manipulation to give them the "general idea" of what to do.

[20] Pearl Berlin, "The Learning of Swimming by Senior Citizens" (a research project cosponsored by the UAW Recreation Department and Wayne State University, Division of Health and Physical Education, October 20, 1960).

Let the beginner shake himself down naturally before the ball and hit. Till he has done this for a good many days, no advice has either use or meaning.[21]

As to the verbal instruction itself, one must distinguish between (1) directions as to how to perform the skill, (2) explanations as to why to perform the skill the stated way, (3) verbalizations which aim at focusing attention on results for more accurate feedback, and (4) verbalizations used for motivating purposes.

Individuals vary tremendously in their individual ways of learning. If the student cannot interpret the language into motor acts, or even into a general idea of what to do, the verbal instruction is ineffective. The explanation of "why" to do it the way directed can have no value in performance except as possible motivation, or perhaps as an understanding which leads to transfer to later similar situations.

In commenting on the use of verbal instruction with the beginner, Ragsdale once said:

> In the beginning do not rely too much on words. . . . He will not understand the directions. He may be able to give you the meaning of every word used; he may be able to repeat the directions; but he has not connected the words with the movements of his hands and body. Directions are just empty words until the pupil has already learned something about the new task, until he has already developed a fair degree of skill. He must first build up a movement vocabulary before he can understand and profit by directions given in words.[22]

If the child can already see his results, as in the act of throwing at a target, for example, verbalization to aid feedback of results may be extraneous and even distracting if carried out while practice is continuing. As to verbalization for motivational purposes, the big problem is whether or not the teacher's words are really having a motivating effect and, if so, on which students.

If some knowledge is involved in the skill, then words may help, but skilled performance must be acquired through practice. When sequence continuities which are not highly integrated occur, words may help the student to link together successive acts. Renshaw and Postle, after experiments in motor learning with varying amounts of verbal instruction, concluded that language was favorable to maze-tracing, or in tasks where the sequence of levers was operated in a specific order, but

> beyond these limits and for other types of skills it may actually impede or hinder progress. The general case in which language inhibits is one in which . . . verbal habits cannot be made effective substitutes for direct sensory stimuli afforded by the task itself. The pursuitmeter, for example, can only be operated by the hands, not by the larynx.[23]

---

21 Sir W. G. Stimpson, *The Art of Golf,* 1887, cited by Mrs. Stewart Hanley in "The Sense of Feel in Golf," *Journal of Health, Physical Education, and Recreation,* VIII:6 (June 1937), 366.

22 Clarence E. Ragsdale, *Modern Psychologies and Education* (New York: The Macmillan Company, 1932), p. 325.

23 Samuel Renshaw and Dorothy K. Postle, "Pursuit Learning Under Three Types of Instruction," *Journal of General Psychology,* I:2 (April 1928), 366–67.

Fleishman and Parker recently studied the factors affecting retention and relearning of a perceptual-motor skill. The task was designed to simulate a complex skill (that of a pilot flying a radar intercept mission). Two groups differing in amount of verbal guidance were used as subjects. The experimenters concluded as follows:

> The most important factor in retention is the *level* of proficiency achieved by the Ss [subjects] during initial learning. . . . The *type* of initial training [amount of verbal guidance] is unrelated to retention performance when proficiency level after original learning is held constant.[24]

Words may help the student at the more advanced level to focus attention on aspects which he wishes to emphasize, although such emphasis is usually a direction of attention toward certain cue perceptions rather than toward the muscular activity itself. However, the advanced student may be helped by certain verbal guides to focus on a part of an act which needs polish or correction.

The habit of many performers of talking to themselves either aloud or subvocally during their own performances is so varied in use and effect that comment is of little value. Some seem to use some kind of verbalism as self-encouragement, some use verbal symbols as linking devices between skills in the unfolding panorama of a sport, and some merely use words as a sort of concomitant emotional outlet.

Teachers are very fond of verbal explanation. However, when talk interrupts needed practice time, *it may actually be a handicap to the learner.* Don't misunderstand this point. Students are quite individual in their methods of learning. Even beginners, especially those who have a background of experience in somewhat similar motor activities, may be accelerated in their learning by some verbal direction. However, this individual verbal guidance should be given in such a manner that it does not reduce the practice time of that portion of the group which has the idea and the purpose and now needs chiefly the experience of trial and revision in attempt to improve. When John Dewey said, "We learn by doing," he could very well have meant any kind of learning. There is an old classroom maxim which states that "telling is not teaching." Both these statements are especially applicable in the motor-skill class.

SUMMARY

In epitome, then, the gross-framework idea may be imparted to the learner by (1) demonstration; (2) manual manipulation (but as a cooperative act); (3) verbal description; (4) movies, loop films, stick figures, or drawings; (5) feeling others perform the act combined with manual manipulation (for the blind); or (6) a combination of these methods. In trying to select a

---

[24] Edwin A. Fleishman and James F. Parker, Jr., "Factors in the Retention and Relearning of Perceptual-Motor Skill," *Journal of Experimental Psychology*, LXIV:3 (1962), 226.

method of orienting the beginner, several points should be kept in mind; namely,

1. Students are different and learn in many different ways.
2. The same student can, with practice and motivation, learn by several different methods.
3. Intelligence, experiential background, degree of motivation, age, functional and structural characteristics, and complexity of the skill, all vary the effectiveness of method.
4. Teachers can often teach best by a method with which they are familiar, providing it is reasonably sound.

certain characteristics of the average beginner should be kept in mind

He is usually easily fatigued. He makes many inappropriate extra movements, and tends to become overstimulated, so that the energy spills over into surrounding musculature and produces interfering tensions. However, this variety and extensiveness of movement is also an advantage in that he more rapidly explores the possibilities of adapted response in many ramifications. Nevertheless, he may fall into basic errors in sound mechanics and persist in them so that, without help, they become handicapping obstacles to the achievement of his true potential.

principles of method

The following principles of method are a synthesis of experimental and empirically derived findings as to what works best for the majority of beginners.

1. Acquaint the student well with equipment and facilities, and introduce the new skills in unified acts large enough to make sense and to serve a purpose for the child.
2. Demonstrate; and repeat at slower rate if he needs further understanding. Blackboard outlines and verbal explanations may not cause recall of sufficient cues from past experience. Follow the demonstration with the learner's practice in attempts to approximate the demonstration.
3. Use closely integrated skill units for *low-skilled* beginners; *e.g.,* throwing, kicking, catching, striking.
4. Diffuse the attention over the total act, with higher levels of attention on the major features of the act.
5. Use a design of performance, or form, in executing the activity which has proved successful many times with previous learners.
6. Use practice techniques for the particular skill which have proven successful in rapid learning for many preceding learners (short, spaced practices, warm-up with lead-up games, etc.).
7. Allow the individual enough leeway so that he can adjust the form pattern to his peculiar structure and unique functional characteristics (different limb lengths, strengths, speeds, etc.).

8. Use constructive guidance rather than faultfinding in teaching the beginner. The free-flowing smoothness of automatic skill does not develop in a tense situation. The beginner needs normal tonus of his functioning musculature and relaxation in the antagonists.

discussion questions

1. In imitation, does the child imitate the gross muscular patterns without thinking about the muscles involved?
2. Does the highly skilled performer of complex skills usually know exactly how he performs the skill?
3. Should the beginner focus attention on the detailed movements of the act he is trying to learn?
4. Is there functioning at various levels of consciousness in learned motor-skill patterns?
5. Do the phrases "seeing with perceptual unity" (Hoyt Sherman) or "getting the gross-framework idea" imply that much of the detailed movement-adjustment goes on below the level of conscious awareness?
6. Does the "gross-framework idea" represent an abstraction of major aspects and a generalization from many preceding experiences?
7. Should the instructor hold the beginner to the precise details of the recommended and demonstrated form?
8. Do the various experiments on sensory limitations (blindfolded, dark room while practicing, "distracting" mental activity during physical practice) indicate that the beginning learner should focus on the precise movements?
9. May focus of attention on, and voluntary conscious control of, movements of a learned act during the attempted performance interfere with unconscious proprioceptive cues which are basic to integrated, automatic performance?
10. Is one's conscious kinesthetic perception identical with proprioceptive facilitation?
11. Should we force hypothetically correct behavior on the beginning learner in order to accelerate his learning rate?
12. Does learning to recognize correct cues and to make correct responses imply that the learner must be allowed to make errors?
13. Does the constant error at the higher skill level tend to be a part of automatic performance?
14. Is verbal explanation the most successful way to give the beginning learner the "general idea" of the skill to be learned?
15. Are there other reasons for the use of verbalization in motor learning besides its use in explanation of how to perform the act?
16. Has verbal explanation tended to be used too extensively in the teaching of motor skills?

V

Motor Learning
at Advanced
Skill Levels

PERCEPTION OF WHAT TO DO;
UTILIZATION OF MOVEMENT PATTERNS ALREADY ACQUIRED

As a background for this chapter, the reader should refer to Hebb's statement, quoted in Chapter I, p. 5, about the nature of the learning of the half-grown or adult subject:

> ... the subject is not learning now to make specific movements, but learning a relationship, an association, between perceived environmental events. This makes adult learning primarily perceptual. ...
>
> Learning at maturity concerns patterns and events whose parts at least are familiar and which already have a number of other associations. ...[1]

The reader should also review the section in Chapter III entitled "Motor Pattern Learning, Especially at the Higher Levels, Emphasizes Perceptual Discrimination and Automatic Action." The adult learner's problems, you will recall, are: (1) perception; (2) movement selection; and (3) integration of these movements into a unit of action. In that section it was pointed out that a large part of the movement selection and integration goes on below the level of conscious awareness, with the attention focused on cues as to "what to do." Learning at the adult level is faster because there is a wide utilization of the previously established repertoire of movement patterns. In other words, there is a difference due to much already available basic body control and simpler individuated movement patterns which can be adapted to the new purpose.

---

[1] D. O. Hebb, *The Organization of Behavior* (New York: Science Editions, Inc., 1961), p. 156; p. 127.

lack of breadth of motor experience
limits possibilities of rapid adaptation through transfer

A distinction should be made here between the learner who has a wide background of simpler skills which may transfer and the individual who arrives at teen age or even adulthood with relatively little experience in vigorous physical skills. The latter at best will have to resort to many of the slower processes of childhood motor-skill learning. Granting differences in backgrounds and aptitudes of various skill learners, we still have great differences in the learning process of the individual learner as he advances from the beginning to the more advanced levels of skill learning.

motor skills grow in generalization
as higher levels are attained

The throwing, striking, catching, and kicking acts of the adolescent who has experienced a variety of vigorous physical activities during his developing years have already developed considerable adaptability. He adapts his throwing acts to stones, sticks, balls, disci, or even trout lines. He has had innumerable experiences in throwing with different distances, different backgrounds of the target, and different implements to be projected. He has kicked many things before he is introduced to the game of soccer. He gradually adjusts his background of throwing to the game of basketball and throws to a teammate or toward the basket. He already has many running, jumping, and change-of-direction acts in his repertoire. He adapts those which seem to be similar to the needs for his new purpose, then refines them to fit more precisely into the new skill.

As the skill develops to higher levels, it gradually becomes generalized; *i.e.*, adapted to the varying backgrounds, the variations in implements, the different playing surfaces, differing opponents, changing weather conditions, or whatnot. A highly developed skill is a skill so generalized that the performer makes the movement adjustments to varying conditions automatically, for the most part, as he attends to the cues for action. High skill level means generalization. Think of the relative impossibility of frequent success in kicking for the goal in a soccer game or shooting for a basket in a basketball game without this generalization. Distances, angles, body positions, one's postural base, physiological efficiency in function, all vary but the highly skilled athlete usually adjusts to these factors automatically in terms of the situation cues. His attention is on the precise cues to guide his action, but not on the action itself.

individual nature and individual adaptability
of learned motor skills

At the higher performance levels, motor patterns for performing the same act become, to a considerable degree, individualistic; *i.e.*, no two persons perform them exactly alike. We acquire motor patterns but we have our own characteristic habit styles. Our walking gait, our characteristic posture, even our highly integrated sport skills are personal and individual habits. However, we need to use caution about the meaning of the word "habit," for it does not imply rigid inflexibility of behavior. The exigencies of the situation, variation in cues and in precise body or object position, degree of fatigue, immediately previous active musculature, even the whim of the moment, all are factors in variation in our *automatic* bodily performance. This statement is applicable although the end results are successful and seem to indicate the same performance.

THE SAME MOTOR SKILL ACTIONS
MAY INVOLVE DIVERSE MUSCULATURE

We speak, throw, kick, strike, or write, with our minds on the cue to response and, at times, on the idea of result. We let the body take over the act while we focus on the cues to response. In fact, we are often focusing ahead for the next cues while the body reacts to those already perceived. Moreover, the desired result of any particular kind of act tends to be approximately the same but the muscle pattern used to achieve it varies. Our gross motor acts—opening a door, throwing a ball, pushing an object— are goal oriented but may be performed by various combinations of our musculature; yet they are performed with the complete automaticity of action which we ordinarily think of as habit repetition. Actually this point is taken for granted in achieving high levels in highly competitive sports. The irradiation of high stimulus (high motivation) causes variations in per- formance and the tapping of unprobed synergistic aids. The higher level learner develops many motor equivalents for performing the same skill so he can change the pattern to offset fatigue or to meet variations in the exigencies of the situation.

The excellent soccer player passes the ball with either foot or with his head, and with innumerable variations in type of pass used and, therefore, in the precise muscle patterns. The highly skilled basketball player is ex- pected to shoot with either hand from many different angles, from different heights of release, from different distances, using different arcs. The assump- tion is made that, at the higher levels, different body acts are available and will be utilized as the cues of the situation stimulate them. Moreover, the successive sport skills, once developed so as to be utilized in the unfolding panorama of a game, are closely associated units but are not habituated into an invariable sequence. Cues from the environment cause sudden changes in the sequential order. The catching and throwing acts are often combined into what seems to be a unified, highly integrated, total response. The action seems to be an automatic response to the cues of the situation. Yet a slight change in cues, a playback from the developing situation, will cause a substitution of different parts in the total act, and a readjusted act which, in itself, often seems also to be a "habit" pattern.

Remember that skills are not specific to the muscles which first acquire them, and that movement patterns but not muscles are represented in the cortex. In other words, one's idea of the moment may stimulate through the cortex a movement pattern, but the muscles which carry out the act vary from performance to performance. Actually the same skill, once learned, may often be performed in gross pattern by completely different musculature. Let us develop this point a bit further.

motor skills are learned by the person, and not restricted in gross performance to specific muscles

It has long been well established that practice of one part of the body in performing a skilled act increases the ability of the bilaterally symmetrical part to perform the same act. This effect has been called "cross education." However, practice also seems to improve ability in various other parts of the body which are not bilaterally symmetrical with the part exercised in the practice. With regard to the first type, Thorndike reported, in a study with adults attempting to write with the nonpreferred hand, that:

> ... the adult starts in writing with the wrong hand with nearly as great facility as the child of eight or nine has in writing with the right hand after two years of schooling.[2]

In 1949 Joanne Black attempted to determine the degree to which the skill of handwriting could be performed by other body parts not bilaterally symmetrical. Her subjects practiced writing with a short pencil held between the molar teeth; and later with the pencil held between the large toe and the adjoining toe of the nonpreferred foot. She measured the quality of the "handwriting" (better called cursive writing in this case) by use of the Ayres Handwriting Scale, and the quantity by counting the number of letters written in each two-minute practice session. Black used practices of two minutes per day for each type of writing. She had her subjects practice ten days, or a total of twenty minutes of practice for the head writing and a total of twenty minutes for the foot writing.

At the very first practice with the pencil gripped in the teeth, 17 per cent wrote legibly. After ten practices (a total of twenty minutes), all subjects wrote legibly with the pencil gripped between the molar teeth. In the foot writing, none of her subjects wrote legibly on the first trial but 83 per cent were writing legibly during the nineteenth and twentieth minutes of practice.[3]

In 1960 Frances Williams did a follow-up study of this script writing with various body parts. Using herself as a subject she practiced cursive writing with the pencil gripped by the teeth, taped to her elbow, taped to her knee, and gripped between her toes. She practiced only two minutes per practice period but practiced twice per day, five days per week for two weeks (a total of forty minutes of practice per method). After completing

---

[2] Edward L. Thorndike, Elsie O. Bregman, J. W. Tilton, and Ella Woodward, *Adult Learning* (New York: The Macmillan Company, 1928), p. 38.

[3] Joanne Black, "An Experimental Study of the Learning of a Fine Motor Skill" (unpublished Master's thesis, The Pennsylvania State University, 1949).

the two weeks of head writing, she started with elbow writing the next week and continued for two weeks; and so on for knee and then foot in that sequential order. Williams makes no comment about whether or not the sequential types of practice affected each other.

Her legibility ratings on the Ayres Handwriting Scale were phenomenal— from a beginning rating of 30 on the first practice of head writing to a rating of 90 (highest rating on the scale) by the thirty-ninth and fortieth minutes. She was almost equally successful in elbow writing but achieved maximum score four practices earlier. Knee writing was legible when she first started and improved in quality rating from 20 (at the first minute) to 40 by the fourteenth practice. The quality did not improve in the last six practices. Her foot writing rose only to a quality rating of 30 in forty minutes of practice, and did not reach minimum acceptable legibility (rating of 20) until the thirteenth and fourteenth minutes of practice.[4]

Although based on only one individual, this follow-up study indicates two points: (1) other nonsymmetrical body parts may take over a skill and perform it very successfully with very little practice (note her head writing in particular); and (2) individuals vary greatly in relative rapidity of adaptability of particular body parts to the performance of skills learned originally by use of quite different body parts. (Williams was much better than most of Black's subjects in her head writing but did not achieve the level of the average of Black's subjects in foot writing.)

Examples of skills performed by musculature not used in the original learning practices are numerous among adults, especially in rehabilitation hospitals. Patients who have lost limbs seem to be able to approximate previously learned skills, at least in gross pattern, with very little additional practice of the new body part used; and they seem to refine the performance very rapidly, providing there is no serious brain or cord injury with consequent paralysis. One extreme example is the Hungarian pistol shooting champion, Karoly Takacs, who lost his preferred arm and then won the world pistol shooting championship one year later, using his other arm.[5]

While performance of a skill by other body parts tends at first to be more awkward and clumsy, the very rapid acquirement of more precise performance by the newly used part indicates that much of the gross-framework pattern has been programmed into the computer of the individual's neuromuscular system, and not just as a habit pattern attached to the specific muscles which did the overt performance in the first acquirement of the skill. However, only the gross-framework idea seems to be carried at the level of conscious awareness. The fast adaptability of the new body part to the performance of the skill indicates a great amount of proprioceptive facilitation which is not registered at the awareness level. Such ready adaptability seems to occur only when the skill has previously attained a high level.

---

[4] Frances Irene Williams, "Specificity of Motor Pattern Learning as Determined by Performance of Cursive Writing by Head and Jaw, Elbow, Knee, and Foot Muscles" (unpublished Master of Education Problem, College of Health and Physical Education, The Pennsylvania State University, 1960).

[5] Ernst Jokl, *The Clinical Physiology of Physical Fitness and Rehabilitation* (Springfield, Ill.: Charles C Thomas, Publisher, 1958), pp. 88–90.

As in all learning of any great degree, motivation to use the new body part is basic to its effective adaptation.

VARIATION IN MOVEMENT COMPONENTS OF SUCCESSFUL PERFORMANCE IN A SPECIFIC SKILL

Variation in the various muscle actions within one skill in consecutive successful performances has been demonstrated in electromyographic studies. This adaptability of the human body is indeed fortunate because identical situations are unlikely to occur in which *exact* repetition is desirable—not that one could repeat exactly the same muscle act even if he wanted to, as is well demonstrated by a person's inability to duplicate exactly his own signature in longhand writing. Identity of signature is considered a proof of forgery (tracing) when such signatures are challenged in court.

less fatigue, less wasted energy, higher motivation at advanced levels of skill

The more advanced student in a particular skill is likely to be conditioned so that early fatigue is not a handicap to longer practice, and hence to more learning. Not only is he in better physical condition for that particular skill performance, but also his relative adaptation to the skill has eliminated many gross, inappropriate movements which were wasteful of energy. He has adjusted his emotional state so that he does not waste so much energy in overtenseness and spill-over of energy into antagonistic musculature. He probably has developed a bit more of whatever strengths and endurances are needed for the skill; hence he has more energy and wastes less of it in inefficient action. If he is highly motivated, he can effectively subject himself to long, gruelling, and persisting efforts with intent to improve.

VERBALIZATION MORE VALUABLE AT HIGHER MOTOR SKILL LEVELS

At higher skill levels words may have meaning in certain aspects of the skill, as means of tying together sequential simpler skills, as means of tying specific cues to specific responses, as means of learning which acts and what variations of previous acts are appropriate for present purposes. Verbal descriptions or explanations, by teacher or from articles written by experts, may be meaningful and helpful. The highly skilled person often has verbal symbols attached to the simpler units or aspects of his motor patterns; hence he can profit from verbal direction emphasizing cues for readjustments and refinements of the feedback of his results. He now understands what it means "to shorten or lengthen his backswing," "choke up on the bat," "keep a wide base and flexed knees," "keep the ball about knee height for the batter on the outside (or inside) corner of the plate," and so on. He has developed, to some extent, a skill vocabulary.

words have meaning in
terms of gross framework

It should be noted that effective skill vocabulary is almost entirely devoted to the general idea of the act, to the gross framework or some aspect of the framework, and rarely to specific muscle contraction. One thinks about lengthening or decreasing his arc of swing in striking actions, of kicking with the foreleg and foot in soccer, of snapping the wrist in handball or badminton, and so on. A high-skill performer often has verbal symbols for aspects of the gross framework to which he wishes to attend; for example, "the peak of the lob directly above the net (in tennis)," when the server is driving him deep and then rushing the net. Perhaps he says to himself, "lob if he drives me real deep for the return stroke"; or "sideline placement if I can play closer and play the ball on the rise."

MENTAL IMAGERY NOT HIGHLY IMPORTANT
IN MOTOR LEARNING

The performer may have a partial image of his own intended act as he prepares to make it; *i.e.,* the pitcher in baseball says he has an image in mind of the path of the ball across the plate as he intends it to go. He sees in his mind's eye, for example, the ball breaking down and out over the outside corner of the plate at about knee height; he has this image of the ball path while he performs the act. Of course, the ball does not always go where he planned.

Warren's Dictionary of Psychology defines an image as follows:

> An image is an experience which reproduces or copies in part, and with some degree of sensory realism, a previous perceptual experience in the absence of the original sensory stimulation.

The amount of such imagery in motor learning and performance is still uncertain. It does seem from experimental evidence that focus on the goal (consciously conceived) is a common procedure and also the most effective one. However, that a clear visual image of a successful performance of the act, as a guide to performance, is necessary or even highly advantageous is not borne out by experiment.[6]

Petro tested a group of subjects on vividness of mental imagery, then had them learn a novel motor skill. He concluded, as a result of his findings, that vivid mental imagery was no advantage in fine motor-skill learning. He found no type of imagery superior to any other (visual, auditory, kinesthetic); and found no correlation between either vividness or the type of

---

[6] "Consciously conceived" does not necessarily imply imagery. Much of the adult's thinking seems to involve chiefly verbal symbolism.

imagery and the amount of motor learning within a specified series of practices.[7]

It should be mentioned that Petro used the same type of *subjective* imagery tests as had customarily been used by psychologists in the past, and that his measures of learning were somewhat questionable. He used inverted, reversed script writing with the nonpreferred hand as his skill, and then used only a quality score as his measure of learning (rated on the Ayres Handwriting Scale). Nevertheless, he stressed speed of writing in his directions to his subjects, and omitted a quantitative measure in his total learning score.

A year later Moody did an imagery study in an attempt to determine the relationship, if any, of imagery differences to levels of ability and experience in motor skills. Moody devised visual imagery tests of an objective nature. Her first test presented geometric figures to the subjects, then, soon after, presented the same figures mixed among similar figures. The subjects were scored on ability to identify from memory the precise figures they had seen before.

Her second test was a series of filmed acts selected from sports and physical education activities. A few moments later the subjects were shown the same precise acts mixed among rather similar acts, and were asked to identify those acts seen previously.

Her third test was similar to the second in its use of films, but the subject was expected to write verbal answers to certain verbal questions about details of the act, as remembered some moments after the brief film exposure.

Moody used female subjects divided into four categories; namely, (1) young, active physical education faculty women; (2) senior majors in physical education; (3) freshman majors in physical education; and (4) freshman nonmajors (students in other curricula).

Moody assumed discreteness of her subjects after (1) selection at widely divergent experience levels, (2) various tests, and (3) a motor-skill learning experience in which relative scores were recorded.

Moody found:

1. No difference among the respective groups in ability to recognize previously presented complex geometric forms.
2. No difference in ability to recognize previously presented motor acts.
3. A difference in answering verbal questions which demanded recall of details of previously presented motor-skill acts; three groups, the majors at each level and the teachers, all did significantly better than the one group of non-majors. The differences among the three groups in physical education were nonsignificant.[8]

The reader should note that it was in verbal response, only, and not in visual identification, that the difference occurred. Recall does seem to

---

[7] Ronald J. Petro, "The Effects of Imagery on the Learning of a Novel Motor Skill" (unpublished Master of Science thesis, The Pennsylvania State University, 1964).

[8] Dorothy L. Moody, "Imagery Differences Among Women of Varying Levels of Experience, Interests, and Abilities in Motor Skills" (unpublished Doctoral thesis, The Pennsylvania State University, 1965).

be tied more closely to verbal symbols than to visual images. However, these majors and faculty in physical education could be assumed to have progressed far enough in many types of motor learning to have a skill vocabulary. Perhaps, also, these experiments are further indications that many important variables affecting motor learning and retention are at the proprioceptive, nonawareness level of behavior. At least, visual imagery does not seem to be a very important variable at the advanced level of motor skill learning.

PSYCHOLOGICAL VS. PHYSIOLOGICAL LIMIT; CLOSER APPROACH TO LATTER AT HIGH LEVELS

One tends to get more enjoyment out of performing a skill in which he has already developed some ability. Moreover, he tends to develop higher levels in those skills toward which he has strong motivation. The problems of motivation, emotion, and psychological aspects of competition will be discussed at greater length later. It is sufficient to say here that the subject at the higher skill level usually is more strongly motivated to excel; hence he drives himself nearer to his true potential. Saying it in another way, what he ordinarily thinks and feels to be his best performance (his psychological limit) approaches closer and closer to his true potential (his physiological limit).

faster cue recognition; reduction in number of cues essential for release of appropriate response

Several other aspects change at the higher skill levels. The subject learns faster cue recognition, and undergoes a great reduction in number of cues necessary to guide the action. He turns his performance more and more over to his body automatism while his attention is far ahead, focusing on cues for the next appropriate action. This last point is familiar to most everyone; for example, the typist focuses several words ahead of her finger activity, the pianist is focusing on the score some notes ahead of the hands' activities; or the student is writing the last sentence presented in the professor's lecture while he is listening to the professor expound his next point.

more highly skilled performer less subject to distraction

The learner at the high skill levels is less subject to distractions; *i.e.,* he can concentrate on what he is doing without letting extraneous stimuli have as much effect on his performance. The fact that so much of his performance is already automatized helps him carry on in spite of distraction. Moreover, he has become more or less negatively adapted to many extraneous stimuli which affect the beginner. He has developed ability to concentrate on cue perception for his activity to such a great extent that many of the irrelevant stimuli from his environment are not stimuli at all to him simply because he does not see or hear them.

Some learners will develop this type of negative adaptation to an environmental situation so that they can concentrate on their reading or lesson assignments in spite of conversation, a radio playing, or other activity in the immediate environment. Many a parent has to speak more than once to his child before he is heard if the child is engrossed in a book, some play activity, or even the television. Sometimes the child may be intentionally ignoring the parent, but often the parent's voice really does not enter the child's field of consciousness because he is so deeply absorbed in his activity of the moment. This type of absorption in the activity tends to develop as a part of higher level skill performance.

"part drill" is more effective and more meaningful at higher motor-skill levels

At the higher levels of skill, the individual can spend practice time very efficiently in polishing weak spots in his performance. The polish of these parts is, at this stage, much more effective with respect to rate of learning because it is not "part drill." The "part" is now a meaningful act because the learner sees its significance in the total pattern, and fills in the rest of the pattern mentally while he overtly performs the part. He sees the part as it fits into the framework of the pattern, even though his overt action consists of practicing a very small part of the total. He is, for example, overtly practicing only a pivot, but mentally for him the pivot is the footwork on the double play pattern by the second baseman, the reverse around the post man in basketball, or the sharp change of direction to be ready for the next stroke in tennis, after returning an opponent's placement down a side line. The learner may also carry out the total pattern overtly but with his attention focused on one special aspect which he wishes to change in some manner. The rest of the act is carried out more or less automatically while he attends to the one part.

THE CONSTANT ERROR AND ITS CORRECTION. The "constant error" which creeps in now and then in the performance at the higher skill levels is corrected in somewhat the same manner. The "constant error" refers to an inefficiency which has crept into performance of a more highly skilled performer, who is unaware of the exact nature of his error. As mentioned earlier, the attention is focused on the error (by teacher demonstration of the error, by a film showing the error in slow motion, by a rehearsal of the error under attention focus by the learner).

The steps in correcting performance of the advanced-skill person who is working inefficiently because of a constant error of which he is unaware are as follows:

1. Have learner rehearse or practice performance of the error itself, with focus of attention on the error.
2. Have learner rehearse the act with the correction inserted.
3. Practice the modification (the correction) together with the total act until the modification becomes united into the automatic-action response of the total act.

Sometimes this process of correcting a constant error seems to the learner very much like starting back again at the beginning of his learning of the skill. However, the relearning of the changed pattern is much faster if these steps are followed than was the original learning of the former pattern. Much of the old pattern does not have to be learned, and the attention can be focused on the aspect to be corrected until it, too, becomes automatic action. This last step of practicing until the correction becomes automatic is very important because, otherwise, the performer will revert to the former pattern under the stress of competitive performance.

SELF-ANALYSIS AND INDIVIDUALITY

The learner at the higher levels of skill can often profit from self-analysis through films and photographs of his performance; he can then experiment with his form and his work method. The strong motives, the persisting, gruelling practice with intent to improve which characterize many learners at the higher skill levels cause the individuals to experiment, to try out and adopt variations in form, training, and practice regimens. The individual learner is more likely to make modifications in terms of his structure, function, and personality. Individual differences among learners increase at these higher performance levels.

A teacher or coach who is an expert in the field, especially one who is well trained in mechanical analysis, may be quite helpful to the learner in guiding his self-observation. However, the teacher who has training in the applied physics of body mechanics but little experience in the skill itself is often likely to overlook certain variables which have to do with the learner's individuality—for example, the running form of Bob Hayes, the fastest dash man in the world from 1964 to 1966, an Olympic champion, and later a professional football player. Slow motion pictures of his fastest races revealed a somewhat wider base, an extreme bunch start, and a bit of lateral body sway during his performances. Questions about this form were raised among some of the academically trained body-mechanics "experts" who viewed the pictures. The expert coaches who handle Olympic men and women are very careful to allow individual adjustments by athletes who have already reached higher skill levels, even though such adjustments vary widely from commonly advocated practices.

The self-analysis and attention to part movements of the total act is often a valuable part of the practice procedure at advanced levels, but this process must be completed and the attention directed away from part-movement focus when the peak performance in competition is expected. Here the attention must again be back on *cues* as to what adjustments to make, the strategy of the situation, etc., but not on the specific movements. The body must now be trained to respond automatically to the cues which the performer is trying his best to catch and turn over to the body automatism for performance. Some of these cues will cause feedback readjustments in action patterns already under way. Perception of the cue flows into automatic response but, as soon as a cue is perceived, the attention focus moves ahead to try to catch the next appropriate cue.

value of mental rehearsals between physical practices

At the advanced levels of skill learning, mental rehearsals between practices seem to be advantageous in several ways. First, they serve as a review of the learner's former procedures, practices, and results and, therefore, as a means for planning more effective succeeding practices and performances. Second, they tend to prevent retroactive inhibition; *i.e.,* to prevent the increase of forgetting, or at least the lowering of performance level as a result of the influence of intervening activities between the practice and performance sessions. The athlete who never thinks of the sport except when he arrives on the field or court is a problem for many a coach. Such an athlete seems to need much additional review and much additional stimulation, and still never seems to perform up to his potential. Of course, it may be that a part of the lowered efficiency is just a lower degree of motivation toward peak performance. Perhaps he has not "gotten himself ready" for peak performance.

The learner who is rehearsing his activities mentally during intervals between physical practice will consider his experiments in form and procedure and their respective results. Such mental rehearsal, and the underlying concern for higher levels of performance, occasionally bring forth new ideas to the learner which, tried out in practice, produce an improvement. In other words, this underlying concern tends to incubate ideas for modifications or changes which occasionally prove quite valuable as an aid to better performance. This incubation is the process mentioned earlier as creative imagination.

fluctuation and last-minute skill review

The individual at any skill level will tend to fluctuate in levels of performance. At the high skill level, the learner will tend to practice not only longer but also more frequently than the beginner. His purpose is now not merely to improve, but also to decrease the amount of fluctuation in performance. Moreover, at the high skill levels, much practice and constant polish is essential just to preserve the level now attained. He not only practices daily, but he reviews his skills for each performance by a pre-contest rehearsal; he insists on a few strokes (or throws) of review after any rest interval, if such review is permitted (five "warm-up" pitches at the start of each inning in baseball, for example). This pre-contest review is ordinarily called a warming-up procedure, but it is more than that. The muscular warmth and body flexibility are important, but so are the fine precisions and adjustments within the skill itself, which seem to profit from this last-minute review.

SUMMARY

1. Advanced motor-skill learning emphasizes perception of what to do, and much of the basic movement adjustment is transferable from previous experience. The integration of movement patterns is largely bodily adjustment below the focus of conscious attention. The attention is focused on cues as to what to do, and the bodily adaptations are gradually acquired from feedback of results and proprioceptive adjustments. The amount of transfer, hence rate of attaining higher levels, is much less for learners who rank low in physical activity backgrounds.

2. Motor skills become generalized as learners advance to the higher levels; *i.e.*, the skills become more and more adaptable to variation in the performance situation and environment.

3. The most efficient form, work method, and practice procedure tend to vary with the individual. Within the same individual, his design of performance and his precise muscle contractions continually vary even though the overt act is successful and achieves what seems to be an identical result. At higher levels, the motor skill does not rest only in the muscles which were used in acquiring it but may be performed, at least in gross pattern, by use of other body parts.

4. The learner at the higher skill levels is somewhat conditioned for that skill, hence less easily fatigued; he makes fewer inappropriate movements; and he has less spill-over of energy to muscles antagonistic to the performing muscles (less overtenseness). He has, therefore, more energy to spend in learning practice and in performance.

5. He begins to acquire a skill vocabulary which helps him (a) in understanding instruction, (b) in clarifying his skill framework, (c) in tying together smaller units which are not highly integrated, (d) in mental planning and rehearsal, and (e) in retention.

6. His learning rate and retention of the skill do not seem to be dependent on his ability to retain vivid, conscious mental images of the desired performance.

7. His higher motivation at the higher skill levels decreases the distance between what he thinks or feels he can do (psychological limit) and what he is actually able to do (physiological limit).

8. At the higher levels he learns to recognize cues for action more quickly, and to need fewer cues to release appropriate action.

9. He becomes negatively adapted to extraneous stimuli; *i.e.*, less easily distracted.

10. Drill on parts to polish certain weaknesses is now whole learning because he fills in mentally the rest of the act as he practices the part; hence part drill is meaningful and conducive to more rapid learning.

11. Serious errors at advanced levels tend to be constant errors, with the performer unaware of the exact nature of them. They have to be brought to the level of conscious awareness, a correct part substituted, and the new part practiced within the whole unit until it becomes a part of automatic performance.

12. Self-analysis during practice, with instructor help and mechanical aids, often accelerates improvement at the higher levels. The analysis must be tried out

experimentally in practice; and any modifications in performance which prove valuable must be automatized before being utilized in situations demanding peak performance.

13. Better results seem to obtain when highly skilled and conscientious performers are allowed considerable leeway in form adjustments to suit their individuality.

14. The learner at the higher skill levels can profit more from mental rehearsal between practices—to review former procedures and results, to plan subsequent practices accordingly; and to prevent forgetting or lapses in mental alertness.

15. The performer at higher levels needs to review (physically) his performance very frequently, not only in an attempt to improve but also just to maintain this higher level once it has been reached. Moreover, he finds it very helpful to review his skills just before competitive performance (before the contest, between halves, or innings, etc.) These last moments of review practice seem to decrease downward fluctuation, and seem to add the final polish needed for a precise performance.

discussion questions

1. Does the very nature of the learning of the adult differ from that of the young child?

2. Is the versatile athlete's ready adaptability to the learning of a new skill merely evidence of another specific aptitude?

3. May rate of later motor-skill learning at adulthood be increased by quantity and breadth of motor-skill experience during childhood and adolescence?

4. Are high-level performances of motor skills quite precise in exact duplication of movements each time they are performed?

5. Can the highly skilled performer execute successfully what seems to be the same skilled act—scoring a goal, hitting the baseball, volleying the opponent's return—in many different ways?

6. Does the retention of a motor skill, once it is acquired, rest only in the musculature which practiced the skill?

7. Are the tension of the highly skilled athlete and of the novice equally likely to spill over into the antagonistic musculature during exacting performance?

8. Does the motor-skill learner tend to introduce verbal cues into his motor-learning patterns?

9. Is skill vocabulary largely limited to gross-framework symbolism?

10. Is visual imagery a basic essential for high motor-skill development?

11. Do psychological limits tend to inhibit the individual from achieving his true potential?

12. In general, is the highly skilled athlete more easy to distract during performance than the individual of lower skill level?

13. Is part drill more effective at advanced skill levels?

14. Is the constant error of the highly skilled performer usually an unconscious error?

15. Do individual differences in form decrease among performers as they become more highly skilled?

16. Should the teacher or coach change the form of the superior performers who seem to be violating certain basic mechanical principles?

17. Is mental rehearsal between physical practices often very valuable at the high skill level?

18. Should the last few minutes of the practice of the skills, just before an important contest, be eliminated lest they "take the edge off" the individual's performance in the contest?

VI

Practice and Factors Affecting Its Influence on Motor Learning

PRACTICE NO GUARANTEE OF LEARNING

In the learning of motor skills, practice sets the stage for other factors to take effect, but practice in itself is no guarantee of improvement. One basic necessity is intent to improve, but even practice with intent to improve may not produce observable learning in certain cases, such as those involving inefficient form, a constant error, or even the actual approach to a high skill level. One practices handwriting most of his life, yet his handwriting has probably long since ceased to improve, and may gradually have become somewhat less legible. Moreover, mere practice for entertainment or recreation does not tend to stimulate much improvement. In fact, if one is satisfied to perform without striving to improve, he is unlikely even to maintain whatever level he has already achieved. In competitive performance, practice against inferior, unchallenging opponents may cause deterioration of performance or, at best, habituation in mediocre performance. If the skill is such that knowledge of results is difficult to determine, the subject may be unguided in his adjustments, hence learn little or nothing. The effect of precise knowledge of results and feedback for adjustment will be discussed later.

practice at high skill levels for maintenance and for generalization of the skill

Much practice at high skill levels is done to maintain the level, with little expectation of much improvement. In academic areas, practice beyond immediate ability to respond correctly is called overlearning and drill, and is done to insure greater retention over longer periods of time. Besides the establishment of the skill (retention), the use of this practice with regard to motor skills, beyond the stage at which successful performance has been achieved, has an additional purpose, although the difference may be more qualitative than quantitative. This additional purpose is the one discussed earlier under "generalization." In motor skills of a complex nature, much practice is essential to increase the adaptability of the skill to the innumerable changes in environment, in opponents, in courts, fields, and equipment, and even in the subject's own physiological condition. It takes practice in many varied situations to generalize the skill so that automatic performance results in spite of varying environmental cues.

FACTORS AFFECTING MOST EFFICIENT LENGTH OF PRACTICE AND LENGTH OF INTERVALS BETWEEN PRACTICES

Let us assume that the level of a skill is far enough below the individual's potentiality for development so that he has much to learn before reaching his potential; and let us further assume that the individual is motivated to practice toward improvement. Several questions now arise as to the practice itself: How long should the individual practice without a rest interval? How long should the rest interval between practices be? The answers to these questions vary with (1) the age of the learner; (2) the complexity and the strenuousness of the skill; (3) the specific purpose of the particular practice; (4) the level of learning already attained; (5) the experiential background of the learner; and (6) the total environmental conditions, including other demands and distractions, activity between practices, and other factors.

With regard to the first of these, *the age of the learner,* span of attention for effective practice on one skill seems to be shorter for children than for older persons. As to the second point, *complexity and strenuousness,* fatigue limits the effectiveness of long practice sessions, and complexity involves the problem of reactive inhibition—trying to cover too great a scope and to persist too long will cause some interference and confusion. The third point, *specific purpose,* refers to the immediate objective of the practice; i.e., whether the immediate purpose is a quick overview of the complex skill for an impending performance, an intense polish of a weak aspect, the correction of a constant error, the development of additional speed or additional endurance in certain aspects of the skill, or some other aim. As to the fourth point, *the level of learning already attained,* fatigue is likely to be more of a problem at lower levels, as is span of time during which the learner can concentrate on and be motivated toward the practice. As was mentioned in the last chapter, longer practices characterize high-skill level performers.

The fifth point, *experiential background of the learner,* concerns variations in physical condition, in applicable simpler skills, and in length of time one can concentrate on and remain motivated toward the practice. The variable of "experiential background of transferable skills" is the one which has not been taken into account in some recent studies claiming the learning of motor skills entirely by mental practice. The value of mental practice seems to increase somewhat as greater heights and varieties of skills are acquired.

Finally, as to *total environmental conditions,* many factors are included. The serious academic student, for example, cannot devote as much time to effective practice as the nonschool amateur or the professional. The weather and temperature may be limiting factors in length of effective practice.

length of practice

There have been numerous studies on most effective length of practice periods. However, many studies of the effects of practice have been done on laboratory apparatus such as pursuit rotors, mirror drawing or star tracing apparatus, chain assembling, and reaction time apparatus. In general, the time span of such studies, both of practice and of intervening rest periods, is relatively short. To just what extent one should apply the findings of such laboratory studies of these fine motor skills to the gross and complex activities of physical education is difficult to say. The findings of several of these fine-skill studies will be presented briefly.

Henshaw and Holman,[1] using various groups and varying the lengths of practice on a chain assembly skill, concluded that extending the daily training period beyond a certain length had no apparent effect on the amount of learning. From experiments with mirror tracing Harmon and Oxendine [2] reported that the relatively longer practices were superior in the first three practices. Riopelle,[3] in a learning study involving complex reaction time, reported increasing superiority of shorter daily practices over longer ones as the experiment was continued. Oxendine,[4] in a mirror tracing experiment, reported that a constant practice length was superior to increasingly longer and to increasingly shorter practice sessions.

In pursuit rotor learning studies, Duncan [5] reported that shorter practice sessions produced more learning in spite of less total practice time. Denny, Frisbey, and Weaver [6] reported that distributed practices produced more learning than the massing of practices. Travis,[7] experimenting with various

[1] Edna M. Henshaw and P. G. Holman, "A Note on Over-Training," *British Journal of Psychology,* XX:4 (April 1930), 333–35.

[2] John M. Harmon and Joseph B. Oxendine, "Effects of Different Lengths of Practice in Learning a Motor Skill," *Research Quarterly,* XXXII:1, Part 1 (March 1961), 34–41.

[3] Arthur J. Riopelle, "Psychomotor Performance and Distribution of Practice," *Journal of Experimental Psychology,* XL:3 (June 1950), 390–95.

[4] Joseph B. Oxendine, "Effect of Progressively Changing Practice Schedules on the Learning of a Motor Skill," *Research Quarterly,* XXXVI:3 (October 1965), 307–15.

[5] Carl B. Duncan, "The Effect of Unequal Amounts of Practice on Motor Learning Before and After Rest," *Journal of Experimental Psychology,* XLII:4 (October 1951), 257–64.

[6] M. Ray Denny, Norman Frisbey, and John Weaver, Jr., "Rotary Pursuit Performance Under Alternate Conditions of Distributed and Massed Practice," *Journal of Experimental Psychology,* XLIX:1 (January 1955), 48–54.

[7] Roland C. Travis, "Length of the Practice Period and Efficiency in Motor Learning," *Journal of Experimental Psychology,* XXIV:3 (March 1939), 339–45.

practice lengths, concluded that the last half of the longer practices was wasted time. Ammons and Willig,[8] concluded that longer practice sessions led to poorer performance of the skill.

A few older studies attempted to throw light on specific public school problems. Fowler D. Brooks [9] reported a study of improvement in the skill of handwriting, involving 184 pupils in three schools. The time span for the study was four-and-a-half months. The pupils in one school practiced handwriting fifty minutes each week; those in the second school practiced seventy-five minutes each week; and those in the third school practiced one hundred minutes each week. Brooks reported that the fifty minutes per week gave as good results as the other two longer practice schedules.

Pyle [10] ran an experiment on the learning of typewriting by nine women and one man, seniors and graduate students in college. Five subjects practiced ten half-hour periods per day with a half-hour rest between practices. They continued this schedule for nine successive days. The other five subjects practiced two half-hours per day with the same rest interval between their two practices. They continued this schedule for forty-five days. Each group had a total of forty-five hours of practice. Pyle reported that he found no significant difference in the amount of learning from these respective practice schedules. (The reader should note the age of Pyle's subjects.)

Pyle [11] also reported another study in which he had four subjects practice transcription of a new alphabet. He had them practicing daily, but varied the length of practice as follows: (1) fifteen minutes; (2) thirty minutes; (3) forty-five minutes; and (4) one hour. He reported that the subject practicing only thirty minutes per day was the most successful in spite of the differences in total practice times. (The reader should note the smallness of the sample.) In the second part of his experiment, he had three of his subjects practice half-hour sessions with rest intervals, but massed into one day. One subject practiced a total of five hours, a second practiced six, and the third practiced six-and-a-half hours. The fourth subject practiced only four spaced half-hour periods that day. Pyle reported that this last subject, practicing only a total of two hours, achieved almost as much as the other subjects who worked most of the day.

The distinction is not always made in the experimental literature between the length of the practice sessions, and the closeness with which practices are clustered in the time schedule. Some experimenters call long sessions "massed practice," while others use this term to refer to a series of sessions with relatively short rest periods between them. The length of

---

[8] Roy B. Ammons and Leslie Willig, "Acquisition of Motor Skill: IV. Effects of Repeated Periods of Massed Practice," *Journal of Experimental Psychology,* LI:2 (February 1956), 118–26.

[9] Fowler D. Brooks, "Time Assignment and Rate of Improvement in Handwriting," *Journal of Educational Psychology,* X:7 (September 1919), 350–53.

[10] W. H. Pyle, "Concentrated versus Distributed Practice," *Journal of Educational Psychology,* V:5 (May 1914), 247–58.

[11] W. H. Pyle, "Economical Learning," *Journal of Educational Psychology,* IV:3 (March 1913), 148–58.

any one session of practice concerns the problem of how long the subject can continue practicing advantageously as far as improvement is concerned. In synthesizing available evidence as to practice length, one might say:

1. For the average person in the earlier stages of learning, relatively short practice sessions are more profitable in terms of minutes of practice. Extra length added to such practice sessions seems to produce no more learning, and may even decrease the total amount of learning. Children in particular seem to obtain no profit from the additional time in the longer practice sessions. However, in some types of skills, adults may increase frequency and length of practices in order to acquire skill in a shorter calendar time. The learning per unit of time is not so great but the additional hours of practice permit an earlier date of mastery. Practices can be too short or too long and only experience with the particular skill and learner will indicate the most profitable length.

2. Relatively constant lengths of practice sessions seem to produce more learning than regular increases or regular decreases in length of succeeding sessions.

3. Short interspersed rest periods within the practice session seem to increase the amount of learning.

4. Adults who are in need of acquiring the skill in a short time can practice profitably many hours per day if the practice is interspersed with frequent rest periods, and if it is not an activity which demands great physical effort. The relative inefficiency of the longer practices is not so great for them, and they may not have the time to spread the practice over several weeks or months.

distribution of practice

The length and frequency of rest periods are also factors which affect learning rates. A few experiments on frequency and distribution will be presented.

In studies utilizing the pursuit rotor, Irion [12] found superiority of learning when rest intervals were interspersed within the practice. Hilgard and Smith [13] reported that distributed practice was consistently better than massed practice. Doré and Hilgard [14] reported that the massing of practice was a greater disadvantage in later practices than in the first few. From two studies Ammons [15] reported that approximately one to two minutes between trials was the most effective rest interval, and that massing produced as much learning as five-minute rests between trials.

[12] Arthur L. Irion, "Reminiscence in Pursuit-Rotor Learning as a Function of Length of Rest and of Amount of Pre-Rest Practice," *Journal of Experimental Psychology,* XXXIX:4 (August 1949), 492–99.

[13] Ernest R. Hilgard and M. B. Smith, "Distributed Practice in Motor Learning: Score Changes Within and Between Daily Sessions," *Journal of Experimental Psychology,* XXX (February 1942), 136–46.

[14] Leon R. Doré and Ernest R. Hilgard, "Spaced Practice as a Test of Snoddy's Two Processes in Mental Growth," *Journal of Experimental Psychology,* XXIII:4 (October 1938), 359–74.

[15] Robert B. Ammons, "Acquisition of Motor Skill: III. Effects of Initially Distributed Practice on Rotary Pursuit Performance," *Journal of Experimental Psychology,* XL:6 (December 1950), 777–87; Effect of Distribution of Practice on Rotary Pursuit Hits," *Journal of Experimental Psychology,* XLI:1 (January 1951), 17–22.

Franklin and Brozek,[16] in an experiment involving gross bodily reaction time and pattern tracing, reported that strictly regulated practice was not absolutely necessary; and that intensive training could be undertaken without loss of effectiveness. Tsao,[17] using mirror drawing as the skill, reported that no advantage resulted from distribution of practice in the early stages, and that massing produced more of a disadvantage later on. Nance,[18] using as the skill a complex coordination task, reported distributed practice to be best for both paced and unpaced work. Kientzle,[19] using inverted writing as the skill, reported distributed practice to be superior, both with earlier and with later practices. Ryan,[20] using a balance skill on a stabilometer, reported a detrimental effect from massing practice.

Massey,[21] using the tracing of a six-sided star as the skill, distributed the practices of her three groups as follows: Monday, Wednesday, and Friday for fifteen practices; Monday through Friday for twenty-five practices; and practices twice on the first day, then once on days 2, 3, 5, 8, 13, 21, and 34, for a total of nine practices. She found no difference in the three groups at their respective ninth practice sessions. At the end of the experiment her Monday through Friday group was slightly better than her Monday, Wednesday, and Friday group. She says the summation plan of the third group takes too much time for learning.

Harmon and Miller [22] reported somewhat different findings from those of Massey. They used the skill of billiards with four groups practicing as follows: daily for nine days; three days per week for three weeks; once per week for nine weeks; and once on days 1, 2, 5, 8, 13, 21, 34, and 55. They report that the only significant superiority among the various practice distributions occurred in the last distribution, and it did not appear until the sixth practice.

Knapp and Dixon [23] completed a practice distribution study with seventy college senior men as subjects, using the skill of three-ball juggling. This study was later replicated with high school students by Knapp, Dixon, and

---

16 Joseph C. Franklin and Josef Brozek, "The Relation Between Distribution of Practice and Learning Efficiency in Psychomotor Performance," *Journal of Experimental Psychology,* XXXVII:1 (February 1947), 16–24.

17 J. C. Tsao, "Shifting of Distribution of Practice in Mirror Drawing," *Journal of Experimental Psychology,* XL:5 (October 1950), 639–42.

18 Roy D. Nance, "The Effects of Pacing and Distribution on Intercorrelations of Motor Abilities," *Journal of Experimental Psychology,* XXXVII:6 (December 1947), 459–72.

19 Mary J. Kientzle, "Properties of Learning Curves under Varied Distributions of Practice," *Journal of Experimental Psychology,* XXXVI (June 1946), 187–211.

20 E. Dean Ryan, "Prerest and Postrest Performance on the Stabilometer as a Function of Distribution of Practice," *Research Quarterly,* XXXVI:2 (May 1965), 197–204.

21 Dorothy M. Massey, "The Significance of Interpolated Time Intervals on Motor Learning," *Research Quarterly,* XXX:2 (May 1959), 189–201.

22 John M. Harmon and Arthur E. Miller, "Time Patterns in Motor Learning," *Research Quarterly,* XXI:3 (October 1950), 182–87.

23 Clyde G. Knapp and W. Robert Dixon, "Learning to Juggle: I. A Study to Determine the Effect of Two Different Distributions of Practice on Learning Efficiency," *Research Quarterly,* XXI:3 (October 1950), 331–36.

Lazier.[24] One group practiced five minutes daily and the other group practiced fifteen minutes every other day. The subjects practiced until they could make 100 successive catches. For the college men, one minute of practice on the daily session was the equivalent of one-and-eight-tenths minutes of the longer, alternate day practice session. The findings with the high school groups were similar (one minute was equivalent to 1.78 minutes).

Cozens [25] reported, in a study of class work in track and field, that he found three practices per week, one hour each, extending over an entire school year, to be better than six practices per week, one hour each, for one semester.

Stull [26] completed studies relative to quantity and distribution of practice, using swimming and bowling as his skills. He measured skill in swimming by speed tests and by the number of strokes learned. His groups in both swimming and bowling were able to develop as much skill in three weeks of six practices per week as the other groups were able to develop in six weeks of three practices per week. As to endurance swimming (long distance), he found different results. The three-times-per-week practices produced as much ability in endurance swimming as the six sessions per week. It should be noted that Stull started in each case with novice subjects.

Scott [27] reported that four days per week were better than two or three in learning swimming. Niemeyer [28] reported that thirty minutes of practice, three times per week, were superior to sixty minutes, twice per week, in teaching swimming, badminton, and volleyball. (Note that the twice-per-week groups also had thirty more minutes of practice per week.)

Young [29] reported a study of archery and badminton in which groups which practiced four days per week for six weeks were compared with groups practicing two days per week for twelve weeks. She reported that the more concentrated practice was best for archery and the more widely dispersed practice best for badminton.

epitome

The majority of the experiments seem to indicate that, at least for gross motor skills, short daily practices are superior to longer practices more widely

---

[24] Clyde G. Knapp, W. Robert Dixon, and Murney Lazier, "Learning to Juggle: III. A Study of Performance by Two Different Age Groups," *Research Quarterly,* XXIX:1 (March 1958), 32–36.

[25] Frederick W. Cozens, "A Comparative Study of Two Methods of Teaching Class Work in Track and Field Events," *Research Quarterly,* II:4 (December 1931), 75–79.

[26] G. Alan Stull, "Relationship of Quantity and Distribution of Practice to Endurance, Speed, and Skill Development by Beginners" (unpublished Doctoral thesis, The Pennsylvania State University, 1961).

[27] M. Gladys Scott, "Learning Rate of Beginning Swimmers," *Research Quarterly,* XXXVI:1 (March 1954), 91–99.

[28] Roy K. Niemeyer, "Part versus Whole Methods and Massed versus Distributed Practice in the Learning of Selected Large Muscle Activities," *62nd Proceedings of the College Physical Education Association,* New York, December 28–30, 1958 (Washington, D.C.: The American Association for Health, Physical Education, and Recreation, 1959), pp. 122–25.

[29] Olive G. Young, "Rate of Learning in Relation to Spacing of Practice Periods in Archery and Badminton," *Research Quarterly,* XXV:2 (May 1954), 231–43.

distributed. In certain types of activities, short practices may effectively be scheduled more frequently than once per day, providing rest intervals are interposed, and providing the activity is not highly exhausting. Various other distributions with increasingly longer rest intervals have been tried. Massey's comment that it takes the subjects too long to learn if their rest intervals extend over several days seems appropriate. The factor of *how soon* the subjects want to have the skill available for use might determine whether or not the same practice time should be more widely distributed.

MENTAL PRACTICE

Mental practice was discussed briefly in the preceding chapter with regard to learning at high skill levels. Many contradictory findings have been reported as to the value of mental practice. Part of the confusion arises over the use of highly unreliable tests. Another point of confusion is the definition of motor learning. If the so-called skill is just an easy succession of simpler skills already learned by the subjects, they often can arrange the order mentally, then put them together in a gross approximation of the pattern by physical performance. This type of procedure is not much different from what ones does when he reads the directions and then puts together some new household equipment or the children's complex electric trains at Christmas; nor is it different from the teaching of the rifle assembly from projected sound films as practiced by the armed services. This "thinking through" is a verbal process to a great extent. One does this kind of learning when he finds his way across a strange city from verbal directions and street names. This type of learning is somewhat akin to maze learning, the experiments in which have been largely omitted from this text. As Hilgard states:

> The maze is sometimes included as a skill, but its motor aspects are in fact subordinate to the serial learning of choices, often learned verbally.[30]

Vandell, Davis, and Clugston [31] reported that mental practice was almost as effective as physical practice (using the skills of dart throwing and foul shooting). Twining [32] reported 137 per cent improvement from physical practice and 36 per cent from mental practice (in ring tossing). Halverson [33] reported improvement by both mental and physical practice, but she says that "the mental practice was not as effective as the actual practice." Verdelle

[30] Ernest R. Hilgard, "Methods and Procedures in the Study of Learning," in S. S. Stevens, ed., *Handbook of Experimental Psychology* (New York: John Wiley & Sons, Inc., 1951), Chap. 15, p. 536.

[31] Roland A. Vandell, Robert A. Davis, and Herbert A. Clugston, "The Function of Mental Practice in the Acquisition of Motor Skills," *Journal of General Psychology,* XXIX:2 (October 1943), 243–50.

[32] Wilbur E. Twining, "Mental Practice and Physical Practice in Learning a Motor Skill," *Research Quarterly,* XX:4 (December 1949), 432–35.

[33] Lolas Elizabeth Halverson, "A Comparison of Three Methods of Teaching Motor Skills" (unpublished Master's thesis, University of Wisconsin, 1949).

Clark [34] reports mental practice to be much more effective at the advanced skill levels than at beginning levels, whereas physical practice is quite superior for the novice groups.

Jones [35] reported that he was able to obtain suitable performance of the "hockswing upstart" in gymnastics without physical practice or demonstration. His subjects were provided with written descriptions of the act, a reading of the descriptions plus mechanical analysis by the instructor, and mental practice by the students; but they observed no physical demonstration and did no physical practice. He reported that 56.67 per cent of his subjects were able to perform the skill at the first physical trial. Jones says:

> It is possible for male university students without previous experience to learn gross body skills of a gymnastic nature by a learning procedure involving only the reading of a mechanical analysis and mental practice of the skill.[36]

Jones reports no test at the start of the experiment, hence one can not be certain that his groups were complete novices in gymnastic skill background.

We might safely assume that mental practice is often a valuable supplement to physical practice; that its effectiveness will vary with the nature of the skill being practiced; and that it will tend to be more effective as the learner moves out of the novice stage.

RETENTION AND REMINISCENCE

Eysenck [37] reports that when the skill involved in the pursuit rotor had been well developed (ten weeks' span of time during which fifty practices were conducted), it was retained to a high degree after one year of no practice. He found no relationship between the final learning score and the retention score after one year.

Ammons *et al.*[38] reported a study of long-term retention of a perceptual-motor skill. The skill was a sequential manipulation of a series of controls on a compensatory pursuit task. He used twenty-two groups of male college students, ranging in age from twenty to thirty-six. Some of his subjects were trained to a moderate and some to a high degree of skill. His various no-practice intervals ranged from one minute to two years. He reported that a greater proportion of proficiency was lost by groups receiving less training.

---

[34] L. Verdelle Clark, "Effect of Mental Practice on the Development of a Certain Motor Skill," *Research Quarterly,* XXXI:4, Part 1 (December 1960), 560–69.

[35] John Gerald Jones, "Motor Learning Without Demonstration of Physical Practice, Under Two Conditions of Mental Practice," *Research Quarterly,* XXXVI:3 (October 1965), 270–81.

[36] *Ibid.,* p. 275.

[37] S. B. G. Eysenck, "Retention of a Well-Developed Motor Skill After One Year," *Journal of General Psychology,* LXIII:2 (October 1960), 267–73.

[38] R. B. Ammons, R. G. Farr, E. Bloch, E. Neumann, M. Dey, R. Marion, and C. H. Ammons, "Long-Term Retention of Perceptual-Motor Skills," *Journal of Experimental Psychology,* LV:4 (April 1958), 318–28.

In a study of motivational factors in gross motor-skill learning, Sparks [39] used high school boys as subjects and volleyball as the skill. Sparks reported that the type of verbal incentive experienced during the learning significantly affected the retention of the skill, although he found no significant difference on group scores at the end of the learning period.

In a study involving the skill of bouncing a basketball from the foul line into the basket, Singer [40] reported that distributed practice was better for immediate acquisition but massed practice better for ultimate retention.

Fleishman and Parker [41] reported, on a highly complex tracking test, that the most important factor in retention was the level of proficiency achieved during initial learning; and that long retention was unrelated to the distribution of the practice in the original learning. They tested their subjects at various intervals over twenty-four months.

Fox and Lamb [42] completed a retention study with seventh grade youngsters as subjects, using softball throwing and batting as the skills. They reported that tests after five weeks of no practice (following the learning period) revealed no significant gain or loss, but that tests given over a range of seventeen to twenty-two weeks after the completion of the learning period revealed a really significant gain. Fox and Young [43] reported, from a study involving the skills of badminton, that improvement had occurred (reminiscence) after six and after nine weeks of no practice, in the wall-volley skill but not in the short-serve skill.

Purdy and Lockhart [44] reported a study of retention of five novel gross motor skills by thirty-six college women after nine to fifteen months of no practice. They concluded that the fast learners are better retainers than the slow learners.

Baer's doctorate at Johns Hopkins [45] was a study of relationship of rate of learning to retention in certain motor skills. His skills were ball catching in a cup, card sorting, and a soccer dropkick. For the first two skills the subjects all practiced until they had learned to a certain level, although

---

[39] Jack Leon Sparks, "Relative Effects of Various Verbal Incentives on Learning and Retention of a Gross Motor Skill" (unpublished Master's thesis, The Pennsylvania State University, 1963).

[40] Robert N. Singer, "Massed and Distributed Practice Effects on the Acquisition and Retention of a Novel Basketball Skill," *Research Quarterly,* XXXVI:1 (March 1965), 68–77.

[41] Edwin A. Fleishman and James F. Parker, "Factors in the Retention and Relearning of Perceptual-Motor Skill," *Journal of Experimental Psychology,* LXIV:3 (September 1962), 215–26.

[42] Margaret G. Fox and Ethel Lamb, "Improvement During a Nonpractice Period in a Selected Physical Education Activity," *Research Quarterly,* XXXIII:3 (October 1962), 381–85.

[43] Margaret G. Fox and Vera P. Young, "Effect of Reminiscence on Learning Selected Badminton Skills," *Research Quarterly,* XXXIII:3 (October 1962), 386–94.

[44] Bonnie J. Purdy and Aileene Lockhart, "Retention and Relearning of Gross Motor Skills After Long Periods of No Practice," *Research Quarterly,* XXXIII:2 (May 1962), 265–72.

[45] Reuben A. Baer, "The Relationship between the Rate of Learning and Retention in Several Motor Activities" (unpublished doctoral dissertation, Johns Hopkins University, 1940).

it took them varying amounts of time to reach this level. For the soccer dropkick, the subjects were just given equal opportunity to learn (*i.e.,* the same amount of practice time). He measured the first two groups after six weeks of no further practice and the soccer groups after nine weeks of no practice. He reported a slight but insignificantly higher retention by the fast learners in each case if recall (first raw score on first trial of relearning) or relearning (number of trials needed to relearn the skill to previous level) were the measures of retention used. However, if the savings method of measuring retention were used (number of trials required for learning compared to number of trials required for relearning), the slow learners were significantly better than the fast learners in retention.

Bender [46] completed a study of the relationship of learning rate and retention, using three skills: field hockey juggle skill, volleyball wall-volley skill, and a badminton wall-volley skill. She measured the retention of her various groups after three lengths of no-practice intervals (69 days, 120 days, and 197 days). She reported that the loss method of measuring retention (raw score on last trial of learning minus raw score on first trial of relearning) and the size of the raw score of the first relearning trial (absolute retention) both indicated better retention by the fast learner. However, if the measure were the difference in number of trials to learn and the number of trials to relearn (the so-called savings method), the slow learner was superior. Perhaps certain specific statements will clarify these points.

Although fast learners may forget more than slow learners, they have learned so much more that they are still superior to the slow learners in total amount retained; *i.e.,* they are still superior in the skill after the extended no-practice interval. However, the slow learner needs relatively more trials to learn than to relearn to his former level. Bender also reported an increase in individual differences of subjects with increase of practice except at the high skill level. At the high skill level this difference seems to decrease again. [47]

PART AND WHOLE LEARNING

Some of the differences in reported results of studies of whole and part learning are due to differences in definition of the terms. Let us first agree on a definition of terms. Gates defines a whole as a "definitely segregated, independent pattern which possesses unity, coherence and meaning in itself

[46] Eileen Koper Bender, "The Relationship between Rate of Learning and Retention of Certain Sensorimotor Skills" (unpublished Master's thesis, The Pennsylvania State University, 1961).

[47] Many experiments in motor learning make this same error of comparing difference in absolute scores at various levels; yet it is evident, for example, than an improvement of one-tenth of a second in the 100-yard dash from 12 seconds to 11.9 seconds does not represent the same improvement as the change from 10 seconds to 9.9 seconds. In archery, an inch closer at the outer edge of the target does not represent the same improvement as an inch closer within the last three inches of the target center. Such improvements, although numerically the same (in Bender's case, less), may very well represent even greater degrees of mastery at high levels of skill than at earlier stages.

above that implied by its parts." He says that an aggregation of items with-out systematic relation, either spatial, temporal, or ideational, even though repeated as a unit (such as nonsense syllables), does not constitute a whole. A part is "an element in a total situation which is essential to the meaning as a whole but which loses its peculiar meaning when isolated from the whole." [48] The whole method of learning is the practice of going through the entire activity each time, and using as many of the whole repetitions as are necessary to acquire adequate performance. The part method is the learning of the individual elements of the whole, then learning to combine them into proper serial order.

There are various approaches to the part learning method. In the so-called pure part method, each part is mastered separately before going on to the next. After all parts are mastered, they are then put together as a whole. However, this last step usually involves a very considerable amount of learning before the parts become linked into a unit of automatic action. Sometimes this integration into a unit takes more time to learn than was necessary to learn all the individual separated parts. Moreover, sometimes a part, learned separately, does not quite fit, and a constant error persists in the performance of the large unit.

The progressive part method involves the learning of part one; next the learning of part two; next the combining of parts one and two; next the learning of part three; then the combining of parts one and two with part three, and so on.

Some subjects seem to learn bettter by the part method simply because they are accustomed to learn by it. There may be more delay in immediate success when they start with the whole unit, whereas some success becomes apparent soon when they start with the small part. The required span of attention is of necessity longer when one goes through the entire act each time. Moreover, the teacher may be accustomed to teach the activity by a particular method (part or whole), and may be better at teaching by the method with which he is familiar.

On the other hand, the activity to be learned may be a closely knit unit, hence easier to learn by the whole method; or it may be a complex and loosely organized aggregation of units. This latter type is often best learned by breaking it up into simpler units.

It should be remembered that many team games are not wholes. They are loosely organized aggregations of skills which can be put together in such various orders as the unfolding panorama of the game indicates. Shooting, passing and catching, rebounding, dribbling, and so on, can be classified as some of the simpler wholes which make up the game of basket-ball. These wholes are then developed into higher units of play patterns. One of the difficulties of the part method, with its isolated development of parts or sub-wholes, is that the parts may be developed in isolation in such a way that they do not fit precisely into the unit of higher complexity. Many a boy has learned to dribble as an isolated skill and then has had

---

[48] A. I. Gates *et al.*, *Educational Psychology*, 2nd ed. (New York: The Macmillan Company, 1953), pp. 371–72.

trouble using his dribble effectively in the game because he watches the ball while dribbling. He misses cues for assists, dribbles into clustered opponents and loses the ball, or even fails to realize when he has a good scoring opportunity.

An old study of Beeby [49] illustrates this last point. Beeby was interested in discovering if a movement pattern, when divided into a number of simpler movements, still represents exactly the same movements with exactly the same relation to each other as they have when performed in the whole combination. In his experiment he used a wooden maze-like apparatus and a stylus. His conclusions were that the constituent movements performed as parts were essentially different from what they were in the whole unit; hence he concluded that the whole method of learning was preferable.

A generation ago Grace McGeoch [50] made an analysis of thirty studies of the relative efficiency of the whole and part methods in learning and retention. She concluded from her analysis that these studies did not justify any generalization regarding the superiority of any method, and that the absolute and relative efficiencies of any given method are the complex resultant of the pattern of experimental conditions in which many factors are differentially and reciprocally effective. She listed the nature of the learner and the nature of the material to be learned as basic factors.

McGeoch's viewpoint was endorsed by Gates many years later. Gates stated that "the most effective method of learning depends, first, on the degree of meaningfulness, difficulty, and length of the material and, second, upon such factors as the individual's intelligence, age, background of experience, and characteristic methods of study." [51]

Studies of whole and part methods have used mazes, typewriting, mirror drawing, piano playing, puzzle solving, card sorting, and other activities as material to be learned. The experiments mentioned below, except for Brown's with the piano, will be only those dealing directly with gross bodily activities.

Brown [52] did several studies of methods used in learning to play the piano. In one she concluded that learning to play a score with both hands at the same time was more efficient than the method of first learning by each hand separately. In another experiment [53] she used three different scores. The first was practiced from beginning to end until it was mastered; the second score was divided into units, each unit was practiced until learned, and then the units were combined; the third score was learned by first

---

[49] C. E. Beeby, "An Experimental Investigation into the Simultaneous Constituents in an Act of Skill," *British Journal of Psychology,* XX:4 (April 1930), 336–53.

[50] Grace O. McGeoch, "Whole-Part Problem," *The Psychological Bulletin,* XXVIII:10 (December 1931), 713–39.

[51] Gates *et al., op. cit.,* p. 374.

[52] Roberta W. Brown, "A Comparison of the 'Whole,' 'Part,' and 'Combination' Methods of Learning Piano Music," *Journal of Experimental Psychology,* XI:3 (June 1928), 235–47.

[53] Roberta W. Brown, "The Relation between Two Methods of Learning Piano Music," *Journal of Experimental Psychology,* XVI:3 (June 1933), 435–41.

practicing from beginning to end, and then devoting special practice to those measures in which there were errors. Brown concluded that the whole method was the most efficient except with the difficult scores. With them it ranked second, but the pure part method ranked last in each case.

Shay [54] equated two groups of freshman male students, then taught the upstart on the horizontal bar to one group by the progressive part method, and to the other group by the whole method. In the first method, the skill was divided into the swing, arch of the body, flexion of the thighs, and extension of the thighs. Shay reported that the whole method was superior, and that it gave smoother timing and continuity.

Knapp and Dixon [55] used the skill of three-ball juggling in a study of the efficiency of the whole and part methods. Their learning criterion was 100 successive catches in three-ball juggling. They used seventeen matched pairs of college seniors in one group and twelve matched pairs in another. In each group one-half of the subjects used only the whole method of practice. The other half of the subjects in the first group used what the experimenters called the part-whole method. They followed a fairly rigid pattern of practice, starting in each practice with one ball, next progressing to two balls, and, in several practices progressing to three. The other half of the second group was left free to choose its own method of practice. The experimenters did not find a difference that was significant at the 5 per cent level, but they did conclude that (1) subjects using the whole method tended to attain the criterion most rapidly; and (2) the initial accuracy attained by the subjects using the part-whole method did not have transfer value.

First, McGuigan and MacCaslin,[56] and later McGuigan, alone,[57] conducted studies of whole and part methods in the learning of rifle marksmanship, using Army Basic Training men as subjects. They used 148 men in the first experiment and 200 in the second. The experimenters concluded that the whole method was better than the part method in slow fire for all subjects, but only for those of above-average intelligence in the sustained fire approaches.

In a doctorate study at Indiana University, O'Donnell [58] experimented with whole and part methods in the teaching of tennis. She found only slight differences, but what she found tended to favor the whole method, based on forehand performance and on scores made on the Dyer Backboard Test.

---

[54] Clayton T. Shay, "The Progressive-Part versus the Whole Method of Learning Motor Skills," *Research Quarterly,* V:4 (December 1934), 62–67.

[55] Clyde G. Knapp and W. Robert Dixon, "Learning to Juggle: II. A Study of Whole and Part Methods," *Research Quarterly,* XXII:4 (December 1952), 398–401.

[56] F. J. McGuigan and Eugene F. MacCaslin, "Whole and Part Methods in Learning a Perceptual Motor Skill," *American Journal of Psychology,* XLVIII:4 (December 1955), 658–61.

[57] F. J. McGuigan, "Variation of Whole-Part Methods of Learning," *Journal of Educational Psychology,* LI:4 (August 1960), 213–16.

[58] Doris J. O'Donnell, "The Relative Effectiveness of Three Methods of Teaching Beginning Tennis to College Women" (unpublished doctoral dissertation, Indiana University, 1956).

Theunissen,[59] also in a doctoral study at Indiana, compared whole and part methods in the teaching of golf. His two groups of twenty-four subjects were equated on a "general motor ability test" which raises some question. His groups had ten weeks of indoor instruction and were finally measured by their scores on eighteen holes of play. He states that the group taught by the whole method had a significantly lower mean.

Niemeyer [60] conducted a study of 366 students in three activities: swimming, volleyball, and badminton. Two classes in each were taught by the part method and two by the whole method. Niemeyer states:

> The swimming results showed that the students in the whole method group learned to swim sooner, farther, and faster than those in the part method group; moreover, they showed better form. . . .
> The performances in badminton indicated that overall learning was not significantly affected by the different methods used. . . .
> The performance results in volleyball indicated that the part method was significantly better than the whole method in early, late, and overall learning or improvement.[61]

Lewellen [62] completed a study of whole and part methods in the teaching of swimming to 104 children, ages $7\frac{1}{2}$ to $9\frac{1}{2}$ years. For his part method he used the Red Cross Progressive Part Method. In his whole method he says the total activity was presented to the pupil from the beginning of the learning process. "Practice on any unit by the learner was carried out only as he attempted the total stroke pattern." Lewellen reported that the whole method was superior to the Red Cross method in developing proper form and in developing distance skill.

Godlasky [63] compared two groups of college men learning to swim, one group starting with the dog paddle, then later progressing to the crawl stroke; and the other group starting in immediately with the crawl stroke. He found no difference in learning rates by the two procedures.

Perhaps we should epitomize this whole-part discussion by saying that, generally speaking, the learner should start with a whole or sub-whole, but at least a unit that has meaning for him. The unit should be as large as he can perceive in its gross framework. If the unit is too simple, it does not challenge him and his interest will die. If the unit is too difficult, if he persists and persists without evidence of success, he gets discouraged and quits. He may even build up an emotional block which opposes attempts at the activity, as many children have done after repeated failure in a

[59] William Theunissen, " 'Part'-Teaching and 'Whole'-Teaching of Beginning Group-Golf Classes for Male College Students" (unpublished doctoral dissertation, Indiana University, 1955).

[60] Niemeyer, *op. cit.*

[61] *Ibid.,* pp. 123–24.

[62] John O. Lewellen, "A Comparative Study of Two Methods of Teaching Beginning Swimming" (unpublished doctoral thesis, Stanford University, 1951).

[63] Charles A. Godlasky, "An Experimental Study to Determine the Relative Effectiveness of Two Methods of Teaching the Crawl Stroke in Swimming" (unpublished Master's thesis, The Pennsylvania State University, 1955).

situation. The teacher may make an error in the size of a unit if he tries to start his students off as he would those of high skill backgrounds. On the other hand, the grade school teacher who is weak in physical-skill performance, but is assigned the task of teaching physical education in the self-contained classroom, tends to make the opposite error. She introduces her students to activities which are at too low a level, which lack any challenge for her active youngsters. Gutteridge [64] reported this lack of challenge even in nursery school and kindergarten. She reported after an extensive study that children in the second and third year of nursery school and kindergarten were often unchallenged and bored by the apparatus and equipment.

The unit for learning should be a meaningful unit and should be taught in as close conformity to its applicable use as possible, with application in more complex hierarchies clarified as soon as is practical. When the skill is too difficult and too long, it will need to be broken down into smaller segments, but these segments should be integrated units and should have meaning in themselves. Complex games, for example, need to be broken into smaller units for faster learning, then integrated into more complex hierarchies of more sophisticated use. The so-called "polish of parts" of the more advanced performer is never "part learning" because he sees the part in its total pattern while he is polishing it, and he does his readjusting in terms of what will fit best in the whole activity.

Learning is more meaningful, and therefore more economical, if it can be intimately linked with its application. This statement is not meant to oppose specific drills or part-method teaching, but to emphasize the fact that the student learns an activity more rapidly if he sees the need for it. Organization of the parts into the whole pattern must be a conscious goal of the student even while he is focusing on parts. Even for part polish, when the size of the unit is not too great, it may be advisable to practice the whole while keeping in mind the specific part which needs particular attention. The student is thereby etching in the details of the configuration. The part emphasized receives continual correction from the stress of the whole dynamic pattern.

Understanding of use aids retention, but in motor skills there is no meaningful understanding until the skill unit is used in the context of the purposeful action. There are all kinds of throws, kicks, dribbles, pivots, dance steps, and strokes. What variation or type to use depends on the situation. The individual has not learned the meaning of the motor unit until he knows the adjustment to use in the phase of the activity panorama in which he is trying to act appropriately. The real test of any learning is the ability to use that learning, when needed, in the appropriate situation. The importance of early experiencing of the motor act in the game, the dance, or the stunt for which it was developed, is apparent. This application, this practical use refines the learning and facilitates its retention. One remembers more easily what he has used successfully.

---

[64] Mary V. Gutteridge, "A Study of Motor Achievements of Young Children," *Archives of Psychology* (May 1939), No. 244.

KNOWLEDGE OF RESULTS

Knowledge of how effective one's performance is becoming, as it occurs, of precisely what variations are less successful, and of just what the result of the performance was seems to be basic to learning. Little or no learning takes place without knowledge of results of performance. Bilodeau and Bilodeau stated in a recent summary of studies concerning the importance of knowledge of results:

> Studies of feedback or knowledge of results show it to be the strongest, most important variable controlling performance and learning.[65]

Wolfle states in his summary of research on knowledge of results that "laboratory studies are unequivocal in emphasizing the importance of giving a subject as specific and as immediate information as possible concerning the outcome of his efforts." [66]

Several basic principles as to effectiveness of knowledge of results on the stimulation of learning have been established, such as the following:

1. Learning is proportionally greater as the quality, exactness, and precision of this playback of knowledge of results increases.[67]
2. When knowledge of results is not available, the learner often can improve to some extent by setting up his own criteria from past experience, to help him subjectively approximate his results.[68]
3. With a delay of knowledge of results, performance declines.[69]
4. Performance deteriorates when knowledge of results is withdrawn.[70]

---

[65] Edward A. Bilodeau and Ina McD. Bilodeau, "Motor-Skills Learning," *Annual Review of Psychology,* XII (1961), 250.

[66] Dael Wolfle, "Factors Determining the Effectiveness of Training," in S. S. Stevens, ed., *Handbook of Experimental Psychology* (New York: John Wiley and Sons, Inc., 1962).

[67] Margery H. Trowbridge and H. Cason, "An Experimental Study of Thorndike's Theory of Learning," *Journal of General Psychology,* VII:2 (1932), 245–58.

[68] William F. Brook and L. Norvell, "The Will to Learn: An Experimental Study of Incentives in Learning," *Pedagogical Seminary,* XXIX:4 (December 1922), 305–62; Clay C. Ross, "The Influence upon Achievement of a Knowledge of Progress," *Journal of Educational Psychology,* XXIV (1933), 609–19; Harold Seashore and A. Bavelas, "The Functioning of Knowledge of Results in Thorndike's Line-Drawing Experiment," *Psychological Review,* XLVIII:2 (March 1941), 155–64; Trowbridge and Cason, *op. cit.*

[69] George W. Angell, "The Effect of Immediate Knowledge of Quiz Results on Final Examination Scores in Freshman Chemistry," *Journal of Educational Research,* XLII:5 (January 1949), 391–94; Irving Lorge and E. L. Thorndike, "The Influence of Delay in the After-Effect of a Connection," *Journal of Experimental Psychology,* XVIII:2 (April 1935), 186–94; F. J. McGuigan, Frances Crockett, and Carolyn Bolton, "The Effect of Knowledge of Results Before and After a Response," *Journal of General Psychology,* LXIII:1 (1960), 51–55; Irving J. Saltzman, F. H. Canfer, and J. Greenspoon, "Delay of Reward and Human Motor Learning," *Psychological Reports,* I:3 (September 1955), 139–42; F. V. Taylor, "Simplifying the Controller's Task through Display Quickening," *Occupational Psychology,* XXXI:2 (April 1957), 120–25.

[70] S. J. MacPherson, V. Dees, and G. C. Grindley, "The Effect of Knowledge of Results on Learning and Performance: II. Some Characteristics of Very Simple Skills," *Quarterly Journal of Experimental Psychology,* I (1948), 68–78.

5. Continuous and complete knowledge of results fosters much greater learning than discontinuous and incomplete knowledge of results.[71]

6. Precise supplemental aids (graphs, films of action, etc.), which provide more precise knowledge or make apparent the differences between the learner's performance and those of better performers, seem to increase learning.[72]

7. Feedback of incorrect information retards learning in direct proportion to the amount of misinformation.[73]

KNOWLEDGE OF MECHANICAL PRINCIPLES

Almost all the studies of the value of a knowledge of mechanical principles as an aid to motor skill learning have used beginners as subjects. Judd [74] compared two groups, one given and the other not given an explanation of the law of refraction, in their rate of learning to hit a target under water with darts. He reported no difference in the groups at the first depth experienced, regardless of knowledge of the mechanical principle; but he noted a superiority of the group with the knowledge of light refraction when the depth of the target was changed.

Hendrickson and Schroeder [75] used an air gun instead of darts, but otherwise their experiment was about the same in design as Judd's. They reported that the groups with an explanation of light refraction were superior both at the first target depth on which they practiced and when the depth of the target was changed.

Frey [76] studied the relative effectiveness of a group given an elaborate analysis of reasons for specific forms as compared to a control group without such elaborate analysis, in the teaching of tennis, volleyball, and rhythms. She concluded that the differences in learning by the two methods were negligible.

---

[71] David S. Abbey and P. A. Cowan, "Incomplete Visual Feedback and Performance on the Toronto Complex Coordinator," *Perceptual and Motor Skills,* XI:1 (August 1960), 43–45; Maynard W. Shelly, "Learning with Reduced Feedback Information," *Journal of Experimental Psychology,* LXII:3 (September 1961), 209–22.

[72] John Annett, "Learning a Pressure under Conditions of Immediate and Delayed Knowledge of Results," *The Quarterly Journal of Experimental Psychology,* XI:1 (February 1959), 3–15; Maxwell L. Howell, "Use of Force-Time Graphs for Performance Analysis in Facilitating Motor Learning," *Research Quarterly,* XXVII:1 (March 1956), 12–22; Lawrence G. Lindahl, "Movement Analysis as an Industrial Training Method," *Journal of Applied Psychology,* XXIX:6 (December 1945), 420–36.

[73] Robert E. Morin, "Factors Influencing Rate and Extent of Learning in the Presence of Misinformative Feedback," *Journal of Experimental Psychology,* XLIX:5 (May 1955), 343–51.

[74] Charles H. Judd, "Practice Without Knowledge of Results," *Psychological Review Monograph Supplements,* VII:1 (March 1905), 185–98 (whole of No. 29).

[75] Gordon Hendrickson and William H. Schroeder, "Transfer of Training in Learning to Hit a Submerged Target," *Journal of Educational Psychology,* XXXII:3 (March 1941), 205–13.

[76] Bernice Frey, "A Study of Teaching Procedures in Selected Physical Education Activities for College Women of Low Motor Ability" (unpublished Doctoral dissertation, State University of Iowa, 1947).

Colville [77] selected three principles of mechanics pertinent to certain common motor skills and three motor skills which utilized these principles. For each skill she used an experimental group which was taught to understand and apply the principle, and a control group taught without direct reference to the principle. She found no difference in learning in her respective groups. She then tried the respective groups on other activities in which the principles were applicable, and again found no significant difference in performance levels.

Cobane [78] tried somewhat the same type of experiment in the teaching of tennis. She reported no difference in skill performance by the respective groups.

Nessler, after a study of methods adapted to the teaching of low-skilled college women, made the following statement about the value of knowledge of mechanical principles:

> Skill learning for the poorly skilled is not analytical. A knowledge of mechanical principles may be helpful in analyzing the completed act, but does not seem to aid the poorly skilled in his performance. Poorly-skilled students are interested in the mechanical principles related to skill learning, but are unable to incorporate this theoretical knowledge into their performance of these motor skills.[79]

Broer [80] reported greater success with a group which had been taught simplified mechanics prior to the teaching of volleyball, basketball, and softball, than with the control group which had no prior instruction in the simplified mechanics. Her subjects were two seventh-grade girls' classes.

In a master's thesis at the University of Maryland, Barrett [81] reported, with respect to the teaching of mechanical principles as a part of the instruction in swimming, that *subjective ratings in form* indicated superiority of the group with the knowledge of mechanical principles. Halverson [82] reported in her master's study at the University of Wisconsin that the knowledge of mechanical principles seemed to produce no superiority over a control group without such knowledge (the skill was one-handed shooting in basketball).

Perhaps a word of evaluation of this problem should be added here. The knowledge and understanding of the mechanical principles of the skill to be learned may not accelerate the learning of the skill for the beginners. If

---

[77] Frances M. Colville, "The Learning of Motor Skills as Influenced by Knowledge of Mechanical Principles," *Journal of Educational Psychology,* XLVIII:6 (October 1957), 321–27.

[78] Edith Cobane, "A Comparison of Two Methods of Teaching Selected Motor Skills" (unpublished doctoral dissertation, Syracuse University, 1959).

[79] Joan Nessler, "An Experimental Study of Methods Adapted to Teaching Low Skilled Freshman Women in Physical Education" (unpublished Doctoral dissertation, The Pennsylvania State University, 1961), p. 148.

[80] Marion R. Broer, "Effectiveness of a General Basic Skills Curriculum for Junior High School Girls," *Research Quarterly,* XXIX:4 (December 1958), 379–88.

[81] Mildred E. Barrett, "A Study of the Effect of the Knowledge of Mechanical Principles on Learning Specific Swimming Strokes" (unpublished Master's thesis, University of Maryland, 1957).

[82] Halverson, *op. cit.*

much time is spent on theoretical explanation with consequent loss of physical practice time, the teaching procedure might be well questioned. On the other hand, a knowledge of mechanical principles may have some motivating value. Moreover, majors in the field of physical education will need such knowledge to guide their own selection of the practice form and method of their future pupils. The experimental literature does not cover the value of mechanical analysis for the advanced student, but empirical evidence seems to indicate somewhat greater value at the higher skill levels.

MOVING PICTURES, LOOP FILMS

There have been a number of studies of the value of moving pictures and loop films in the teaching of motor skills. Only a brief epitome will be presented here. First, they are of real value in giving the learner the general idea of the action pattern if the teacher is not completely competent at demonstration. Moreover, they may add to the learner's motivation. Second, slow-motion pictures will sometimes reveal the precise form when the act itself cannot be performed in slow motion as a demonstration device. The live slow-motion demonstration actually incorporates different movement patterns from those used in acts which must be performed rapidly to be functional in normal performance. Third, moving pictures of the learner may help him discover constant errors, and may be quite helpful in form analysis at high skill levels. Moreover, comparison of the learner's performance with the performance of experts may be an added and valuable supplement to the knowledge of his own results. Fourth, time which might better be utilized in physical practice is sometimes wasted in showing moving pictures. Fifth, knowledge of precise results of individual performance in many team games is very difficult to obtain other than by postgame movie analysis, yet such knowledge is essential for rapid learning. However, the films may need to be analyzed by an expert teacher, the material abstracted, synthesized, and then pointed out to the learner. Finally, the extensive use of films, paralleling the teaching and practice of a motor skill with beginners, is of questionable value.

Mention perhaps should be made here of the new types of apparatus which give instant playback television recordings of performances. When available, these instruments make possible the great advantage to learning discussed above in the section, "Knowledge of Results."

discussion questions

1. Is practice in itself the basis of skill learning?
2. Is practice at high skill levels essential just to maintain the high level?
3. Should one attempt to keep all conditions of practice constant?
4. Does the length of practice for most effective learning vary with the skill being practiced?
5. Does the length of practice for most effective learning vary with the level of learning?

6. Does the length of practice most effective for learning vary from individual to individual?

7. Are your answers to questions 4, 5, and 6 equally applicable to length and frequency of rest intervals between practices?

8. Generally speaking, do short, frequent practices tend to be more effective than longer practices, in the early stages of gross-physical-skill learning?

9. May the adult find it advantageous to bunch his practice time into a much shorter span on the calendar?

10. In general, is daily (or five times per week) practice superior to two or three practices per week when total practice time is held constant?

11. Can novel physical skills be learned without physical practice?

12. Does mental practice seem to be more valuable at advanced skill levels?

13. Does the slow learner need proportionately fewer relearning trials than the fast learner to achieve his post-training test score?

14. Do fast learners retain more than slow learners?

15. Is a complex game (hockey, soccer, football, tennis) a whole?

16. Are the teacher, the learner, and the skill itself all variables which affect the relative effectiveness of the whole as compared to the part method?

17. Is it a good hypothesis to say: "In case of doubt, start with the larger unit"?

18. Does meaning in motor skills imply ability to describe the skill verbally?

19. Is knowledge of results essential for significant progress in learning?

20. Is it well established that knowledge of mechanical principles aids the beginner to acquire a new skill more rapidly?

21. Does it seem profitable in the acceleration of learning to frequently decrease the physical practice time in order to show movies of the skill being performed?

VII

Motivation, Emotion, and Stress

The terms motivation, emotion, and stress are used with such a variety of meanings or shades of meaning in the literature that our discussion must of necessity start with some differentiation.

MOTIVATION

Let us define motivation as a state of "being aroused" to action—aroused from passivity or calmness to restlessness, to a degree of dissatisfaction or disturbance, and then to directed purposeful acts. This state of arousal to action, this disturbance of homeostasis, may result from some internal organic or psychic need. Hunger, thirst, tissue injury, and sex are commonly listed as primary motivations. These needs become conditioned or directed through learning into purposes or desires to obtain something or escape from something. *The motive* is then the desire for a specific object or goal, or the desire to escape from a situation or environment.

The individual is activated by many motives, not only those commonly recognized, such as desires for food and water, but also many derived or learned motives, such as desire for money, praise, social status, security, self-respect. He gets to want to finish a job, once started; or perhaps he takes pride in his own workmanship, or in his personal appearance. He seems to have a basic need to express his potentialities and to react to his environment.

Some of man's motivations, perhaps what we mean by psychic rather than organic needs, have to do with his apparent need to be active and to explore and manipulate his environment. These motives are not only almost universal in the human species but are also characteristic of much animal behavior. Much of this type of activity has been characterized as play. As Huisinga says:

> This intensity of, and absorption in play finds no explanation in biological analysis. . . . The fun of playing resists all analysis, all logical interpretation. . . . Here we have to do with an absolutely primary category of life, familiar to everyone at a glance right down to the animal level. . . . Since the reality of play extends beyond the sphere of human life it cannot have its foundations in any rational nexus, because this could limit it to mankind. . . . In culture we find play as a given magnitude existing before culture itself existed, accompanying it and pervading it from the earliest beginnings right up to the phase of civilization we are now living in.[1]

A continuance of a quiescent state is annoying to the healthy human, so he seeks activity. As Cannon says, the individual seems to seek imbalance through activity.[2]

It must not be assumed that these psychic needs are the products of learning, although the direction of their expression in activity involves learning. For example, the human need for affiliation with some of his own kind seems to be inborn. Complete and extended isolation is a serious punishment for the normal human being. Even many animal species display a need for affection, seeking physical contact and cuddling very early in the infant stage. In a famous study by Harlow and Zimmerman,[3] monkeys were raised with two fake mothers, one fabricated from terry-cloth and one from wire; they came to prefer the cloth mother although their feeding was administered through the wire mother. The experimenters say:

> These data make it obvious that contact comfort is a variable of critical importance in the development of affectional responsiveness to the surrogate mother, and that nursing appears to play a negligible role. With increasing age and opportunity to learn, an infant fed from a lactating wire mother does not become more responsive to her as would be predicted from a derived-drive theory, but instead becomes increasingly more responsive to its nonlactating cloth mother.[4]

Motivating conditions tend to focus attention and behavior on goal-related aspects of the situation; *i.e.,* the motive tends to direct the persistent though variable activity and to determine the type of responses which are made. With increase in strength of motive, there is a corresponding increase in energy expended.

incentives

Incentives are external stimuli which the individual likes, wants, desires to obtain. They are devices to get people to do tasks irrespective of any

---

[1] Johan Huisinga, *Homo Ludens: A Study of the Play Element in Culture* (Boston: The Beacon Press, 1950), pp. 2–4.

[2] Walter B. Cannon, *Bodily Changes in Pain, Hunger, Fear and Rage* (New York: Appleton-Century-Crofts, 1934).

[3] Harry F. Harlow and Robert R. Zimmerman, "Affectional Responses in the Infant Monkey," *Science,* CXXX:3373 (August 21, 1959), 421–32.

[4] *Ibid.,* p. 423.

satisfaction inherent in the doing of the work itself. If they are really incentives to the individual, they increase performance of the goal-directed activity. Industry uses bonuses, promised raises in salary, public recognition, or piece-work payments as incentives. In industry the ego-satisfaction of the employee is at times more important to him than money and security. The ego-involvement of the worker crops up frequently in attempts at settlement of strikes in industry. Ego-involvement refers to any treatment which affects the worker's (or learner's) status in his social group or society, his self-pride, prestige, and self-estimation. To some teachers a raise in professional rank is very important even though it does not include a raise in salary; conversely, some teachers have different goals and would prefer to have the raise in salary even if it included a lower professional status.

Common incentives used by teachers in the attempt to stimulate students are praise and reproof, promise of reward, prizes, better grades, rivalry and competition, and ego-involvement. They use these devices in attempts to stir the students to greater activity. It is clear that one must be active to learn; hence he must have some drive and must attend to the learning situation. He must have a set toward learning.

The evidence is somewhat conflicting as to the effect of strength of motivation on learning, but, in general, the rate of learning seems to increase with increase in stimulus. This increase may result from nothing other than the set to learn, the greater attention, and the greater variety in trial attempts. However, there is a peak of strength of effective stimulus for each individual, after which the learning curve drops down. Along the continuum of motivation from mild stimuli through strong stimuli with the more generalized resultants (emotional accompaniment), we have more action, more varied action, and often improved performance up to the individual's particular tolerance, then a drop in performance efficiency, and finally complete failure of effective performance.

EMOTION

The term emotion refers to the accompanying conscious feeling tone which occurs as higher degrees of motivation begin to produce more generalized chemical and physiological reactions. (1) The stimuli, (2) the feeling tones, and (3) certain responses become patterned through learning into what we ordinarily call forms of *emotional expression*. For example, punishment or failure may produce conditioning of many neutral but associated stimuli so that any similar situation produces anxiety and worry. The anxiety and worry feelings are types of emotion. The chemical and physiological changes produced by anxiety and worry (or by any other emotion-feeling, such as irritation and anger) are the body's attempts to restore normal homeostasis. They are the efforts which we call stress. Disturbance of homeostasis, and therefore stress, may also be caused by many other stimuli besides those catalogued as emotional; *e.g.*, cold, heat, disease, tissue injury, heavy physical effort.

Milder degrees of emotional stimulation tend to improve performance and hasten learning. When the learning reaches more advanced levels and much of it is already automatized, a higher degree of emotion can be experienced without loss in performance efficiency and, at times, even with an improvement in performance. However, the nature of the individual, his previous experience with emotional stimuli, and his subsequent success or failure will affect his efficiency of action under strong stimuli. Actually, expression of emotion develops into specific patterns, both in motor expression and in neural action. Emotional behavior in the mature adult often has acquired adjusted responses so that it is only distinguishable from ordinary motivated action by intensity, vigor, and degree of concern. However, it may also have acquired nonadaptive and antisocial responses in the emotionally immature adult. There are some cases on record of performance of feats beyond normal powers after extreme visceral upheaval in the presence of an emergency situation. These are probably not nearly as frequent in occurrence as cases of inferior performance or even of complete inhibition of adjusted action.

Vaughan [5] presents the view that it takes an upsetting experience such as the disparagement of one's ability at the unkind hands of another to remove the inhibitions that circumvent one's expansion; that no one knows how much he can do until he is driven by some excitement to extend himself. Emerson says in his essay "Compensation":

> Our strength grows out of our weakness. The indignation which arms itself with secret forces does not awaken until we are pricked and stung and sorely assailed.

qualitative and quantitative changes with increased intensity of stimulation

Any activity implies drive or motive, but only those involving special feeling tones, visceral reactions, and activity of the sympathetic division of the autonomic nervous system are classified as emotional. Let us assume varying degrees of stimulation, varying degrees of need, varying degrees of disturbance of equanimity, of homeostasis. Under the mild stimuli of everyday living, one may make habit responses or learned adjustments without extreme physiological reactions or strong conscious feelings of pleasure or pain, joy or sorrow, excitement or boredom. One may get up in the morning, eat breakfast, and go about routine duties without experiencing stimuli strong enough to spill over to any appreciable degree into the sympathetic division of the autonomic nervous system. His digestion proceeds while he goes about the other activities of his daily living. He responds to the regular rhythm of organic needs, hunger and thirst, at suitable intervals; and to task responsibilities, family duties, and social obligations by adjustment patterns already learned or easy to construct from his background of experience.

He bids his wife and the children goodby as he starts off to work, with a

---

[5] Wayland F. Vaughan, *The Lure of Superiority* (New York: Holt, Rinehart & Winston, Inc., 1928), p. 113.

kiss or a hug of affection which momentarily stirs him a little deeper—with that milder degree of emotion which we call "feeling." This feeling is usually a mild degree of emotion. However, under the daily habit situation of departing for work, this feeling does not involve a high degree of stimulation. Let us think of emotion as a continuum from mild feelings which only slightly tinge the tempo of ordinary living and are accompanied by only mild additional changes in the physiological processes, to the extremes of vigorous and violent feelings and reactions. We have a continuum from mild anxiety to extreme fear; from gentle affection to passionate love; from mild annoyance to violent anger. The term emotion is used to describe the heightened feeling tone which accompanies stronger stimulus and subsequent disequilibrium, a greater upheaval than what we speak of as ordinary motivation. Our mild hunger motivated us to eat breakfast.

Although the physiological changes accompanying strong emotion may produce some noticeable and measurable changes, the distinction between motivated behavior and emotional behavior is a matter of degree rather than kind. When one's motives are greatly strengthened through deprivation, or activated by internal or external stimuli of considerable strength, they begin to cause deep feeling tones and physiological reactions such as spill-over of stimulus into the sympathetic division of the autonomic nervous system, higher tonicity in the smooth muscles, and a few observable actions farther along the continuum toward emotional patterns of response. Extreme emotion may block out one's hunger motivation, or the physiological changes accompanying such emotion may stop the digestion of the food after it is eaten. The flood of energy-release and the rather profound chemical and physiological changes occurring under very strong stimulus seem to be accompanied and interrelated with a greatly accentuated surge of feelings. These feelings are vividly registered in our consciousness; *i.e.*, we are extremely aware of these feelings.

emotion, a subjective feeling

Some authorities call the extensive physiological changes themselves the emotion; but for our purposes we shall consider the greatly heightened feelings and sensations, of which we are aware at the conscious level, as the emotion. Perhaps the reader has experienced a very-near-accident situation in a car in which his *habit responses* on steering wheel and brake have extricated him from what might very well have been a tragic accident. The emergency responses are over and the situation is again normal in an instant except that, afterward, one begins to feel the surge of emotion, the fear which accompanies the stirred-up state from the sudden very strong stimulus. The strong feelings which we experience under very strong stimulation are apparently a conscious accompaniment of certain deeply stirred physiological states; but whether or not they are always the results of the physiological disturbance is another question. Perhaps the emotionally stimulating situation initiates both the neurological pattern which we feel as emotion and the physiological disturbances; *i.e.*, perhaps they are concomitant occurrences, and perhaps each reinforces the other.

Long ago William James said:

> My theory . . . is that *the bodily changes follow directly the perception of the exciting fact, and that our feeling of the same changes as they occur IS the emotion.*[6]

Let us assume that the rather extensive bodily changes, both chemical and physiological, which we shall list in more detail a little later, *may be* the stimuli for the psychological effect which we experience consciously and label an emotion. But we must not overlook the fact that mental states can also initiate extensive physiological changes. Irritations on the daily job may run up blood pressure and stop digestion. Anxiety and worry are purported to be causal factors in stomach ulcers. On the other hand, play, games, joyous physical activity are advocated for mental health—a form of catharsis to restore emotional normality, equanimity, and equilibrium.

STRESS [7]

The term stress has been used extensively in the literature, especially after the publications of Hans Selye. Selye presents stress as a disturbance of normal homeostasis, an effort to reachieve normal equilibrium after homeostatic balance has been upset. The effort involves action of the sympathetic division of the autonomic nervous system, with its wide visceral and glandular control. The stimuli which cause stress (stressors) may come from physiological or psychological needs or deprivations, or from environmental conditions. Selye divides the stages of reaction to stressors into, first, the alarm stage, second, the resistance stage, and, third, the stage of exhaustion. He defines stress as the process involving nonspecifically induced changes within the biologic system. The body is said to be experiencing stress when it undergoes any stimulus strong enough to cause some activation of the sympathetic division of the autonomic nervous system. Selye states that the resistant stage involves secretions of glandular hormones and formation of conditioned reflexes as defense reactions.

The term stress is used to describe bodily conditions in the adjustment to physical effort, to fatigue, and to tissue injury and in resistance to disease or harmful poisons. It is also often used to describe the stirred-up states of the organism which James felt to be the precursors of the conscious feeling called emotion.

Lundervold,[8] using electromyographic records, reported wider muscle

---

[6] William James, *Psychology: The Briefer Course* (New York: Holt, Rinehart & Winston, Inc., 1893), p. 375.

[7] Hans Selye, *The Story of the Adaptation Syndrome* (Montreal: Acta, Inc., Medical Publishers, 1952); *The Physiology and Pathology of Exposure to Stress* (Montreal: Acta, Inc., Medical Publishers, 1950); *The Stress of Life* (New York: McGraw-Hill Book Company, 1956).

[8] Arne Lundervold, M.D., "The Measurement of Human Reaction During Training," *Health and Fitness in the Modern World* (Chicago: Athletic Institute, Merchandise Mart, 1961), pp. 119–33.

use with: (1) fatigue; (2) stress or stronger stimulus; (3) greater speed. Each of these three factors also produced more tension in the antagonists. Training produced higher speed with less muscular activity according to the electromyographic records. Unpleasant feelings increased the muscular and vascular work. Favorable psychic factors seemed to tend to postpone fatigue.

Hellebrandt, in commenting on the usefulness of certain automatic reactions which emerge under stress, says:

> ... The irradiation associated with extreme stress is so wide-spread that a willed movement limited to a single appendicular joint may evoke action potentials in muscles located in all four extremities, the head and neck, and the trunk. These seem to us to be orderly and wholly integrated total patterns of response. Observing them we get the impression that they are the obligatory concomitants of very severe stress, and the only way in which the highest threshold motor units of the muscle subjected to direct training can be activated. These are the motor units held in reserve and called upon when truly maximum effort is demanded—when you rush into a burning house and perform some phenomenal feat of strength, or when you break the 4-minute mile, or swing your paralyzed legs across a street in the time-span of the green light that gives you the right of way.[9]

The reader will need to use caution in interpreting the literature with respect to stress and emotion, for the terms seem at times to be used interchangeably. In fact, some of the texts have called the deep visceral and glandular changes from strong stimuli, emotion. The definition is unimportant as long as the reader is not confused as to whether he is considering physiological and chemical changes, or conscious feeling-patterns accompanying such changes. Actually, under what would normally be an emotionally stimulating situation, animals show behavior symptoms which seem to be their typical, overt, emotional-pattern reactions *even after their cortices are removed*.

We have used the conscious aspect, the feeling tones, to define emotion in this chapter in order to attempt to distinguish between emotion and certain types of stress. The strong stimuli which cause extensive disequilibrium, internal upset, a stirred-up physiological state, do not need to be emotional in the common usage of the term (intense feeling stimuli). Toxic substances, illness, or tissue injury may also cause extensive chemical and physiological changes in the body.

physiological and chemical changes
associated with emotional stimulation [10]

Perhaps it would be well to mention again several of the kinds of chemical and physiological changes which seem to precede or accompany the subjective feelings which we have called emotion.

---

[9] Frances A. Hellebrandt, "The Physiology of Motor Learning," *Cerebral Palsy Review*, XIX:4 (July-August 1958), 12.

[10] It should be noted that many of these changes also occur in varying degrees in conditions of stress from other than emotional stimulation.

When the sympathetic division of the autonomic nervous system is strongly stimulated, we have a cooperative inhibition effect in the cranial and the sacral divisions. There is stimulus to the smooth muscles and the ductless glands. Digestion is stopped. There is contraction of the arteries which feed the blood to the alimentary canal, and the blood is forced out into the skeletal musculature and into the body's peripheral blood vessels. Blood pressure often increases, saliva flow decreases, perspiration increases, body temperature changes, the heart and respiration rates increase, there is much glandular activity including the release of adrenin into the bloodstream, some changes in blood chemistry including a release of more sugar into the blood, and a speeding up of the coagulation time of the blood.

With higher blood pressure, chemical changes in the blood, faster and stronger heart beat, and faster breathing, osmosis is faster, food and oxygen reach the cells sooner, and waste products are carried away faster; *i.e.,* more energy is available for effort and less fatigue occurs. The body makes these adjustments to emergency conditions, but the direction of these extra powers for performance depends on the individual's ability to adjust and control their expression. Herein previous conditioning and learning experience play an important role.

EXPERIMENTAL STUDIES

Experimental studies in the fields of motivation, emotion, and stress suffer from several weaknesses. For one thing, we can only measure change in performance and then hypothesize that the change was due to the additional factor introduced into the experimental situation. But the experimenter himself is a variable. As one can well remember from his own school experience, praise or reproof from one teacher might have a much different effect than the same treatment from a different teacher. The kind of instruction and the social conditions surrounding the total experimental environment may also affect results.

Moreover, the effectiveness of the stimulus may very well vary with the level of learning already attained. The previous degree of success or failure of the subjects may affect the results. Both age and intelligence of the subjects may be variables. If there is great ego-involvement by some subjects, anxiety over failure may have disruptive effects. Introspective, questionnaire, and projective techniques are at best very subjective measures. When such procedures are not used to measure emotion, some measure is usually taken indirectly by measurement of certain body changes; however, most of the physiological responses so measured are affected by too many other variables to be sure indices of degree of emotional arousal.

In an old but frequently cited study of competitive bicycle riding, Triplett [11] stated in 1897: "From the above facts re: the laboratory races, we infer that bodily presence of another contestant participating simultaneously

---

[11] Norman Triplett, "The Dynamogenic Factors in Pace Making and Competition," *American Journal of Psychology,* IX:4 (July 1897), 507–33.

in the race serves to liberate latent energy not ordinarily available." Competition and rivalry are common variables used in motivational studies. In a study of very young children Greenburg [12] found some competition occurring in the activities of children between the ages of three and four in their various play activities and in their various efforts to achieve recognition or dominance in a situation. There was a gradual increase of competition with age, so that competition had become extensive between the ages of six and seven.

Mehran K. Thompson says of competition:

> Competition and rivalry satisfy basic needs in the individual and the race. We speak of competitive games and often refer to the game of life as such, for, from the cradle to the grave, we are competing for something or other. Competition and rivalry are rooted in the *élan vital*, the evolutionary urge. They constitute the push in the struggle to survive and the desire for supremacy. Competition runs all through life. A man must compete for the means of livelihood, for his social position, for his friends, in fact, for everything which is worth-while. Civilized society has not eliminated rivalry; on the contrary, it has extended the field from the purely physical and biological to the intellectual, social, moral, and spiritual. . . .
> The object is to utilize the advantages and avoid the pitfalls [in the use of competition to motivate school learning.] The advantages are: (1) it provides zest and meaning to life; (2) it is positive and satisfies a basic urge; (3) it builds up morale and ego-maximization; (4) it stimulates growth, development, and maturation; (5) it could lead to self-improvement, for competition can be used against oneself as well as against others. The chief danger is that if competition is too keen, the individual is likely to suffer defeat, frustration, and possible demoralization.[13]

deprivation and satiation

Gerwitz and Baer [14] experimented with children in a simple motor-skill "game." Each subject of one group was isolated for twenty minutes before he started the skill. A second group went directly to the experiment. A third group was "satiated" on the way to the experimental situation by extremely solicitous and approving comments and actions on the part of the experimenter. All were praised during performance. The "deprived" subjects, those who had been isolated, were superior in acquiring and performing the skill; the group that went directly to the experiment ranked second; and the "satiated" group, the group that had had extensive praise preceding the experiment, did the poorest.

---

12 P. T. Greenburg, "Competition in Children: An Experimental Study," *American Journal of Psychology,* XLIV:2 (April 1932), 221–48.

13 Mehran K. Thomson, "Motivation in School Learning," in Charles E. Skinner, ed., *Educational Psychology,* 4th ed. (Englewood Cliffs, N.J.: Prentice-Hall, Inc., 1959), Chap. 16, pp. 465–66.

14 Jacob L. Gerwitz and Donald M. Baer, "Deprivation and Satiation of Social Reinforcers as Drive Conditions," *Journal of Abnormal and Social Psychology,* LVII:2 (September 1958), 165–72.

individual variability in reaction to motivational situations

Almost any experimenter who has dealt with groups of considerable size has found great individual variability in effects. This variability is often not stressed because conclusions are drawn from group means and their differences. Two studies will be mentioned in which attention has been focused on variability. In other experiments the reader can note the same phenomenon if he examines the data.

Birger Johnson [15] compared bicycle ergometer work by junior high school boys under a combination of incentives. His incentives were a competitive situation plus urging and encouragement during the exercise trials. His measures of reaction to "emotional stimulation" were changes in heart rate and blood pressure. He states that the reactions of these adolescents were very variable and that acute adjustments in heart rate and blood pressure indicated greater effort but not necessarily greater total work output. Some boys were able to do more work under the motivating conditions, while others were not, in spite of physiological indications of greater effort being exerted.

Rexroad [16] concluded, after finding a great variety of results from electric shock in continuous multiple-choice reactions with college students, that electric shock punishment had three effects: (1) disruptive, (2) incentive, (3) instructive.

effect varies with level of learning or experience

Fleishman [17] reported, from a study using a simulator of manipulation of airplane controls as the skill and strong verbal exhortation as the incentive, that only the better half of the motivated group did better than the control group. Lazarus and Deese "found some evidence which led them to believe that emotional stress induced early in the learning process, before skills have been well organized, produced a detrimental effect on learning, while stress induced later in learning produced a slightly facilitating effect." [18]

---

[15] Birger L. Johnson, "Influence of Puberal Development on Responses to Motivated Exercise," *Research Quarterly,* XXVII:2 (May 1956), 182–93.

[16] Carl N. Rexroad, "Administering Electric Shock for Inaccuracy in Continuous Multiple-Choice Reactions," *Journal of Experimental Psychology,* IX:1 (February 1926), 1–18.

[17] Edwin A. Fleishman, "A Relationship Between Incentive Motivation and Ability Level in Psychomotor Performance," *Journal of Experimental Psychology,* LVI:1 (July 1958), 78–81.

[18] James Deese, *The Psychology of Learning* (New York: McGraw-Hill Book Company, 1952), pp. 322–23, citing Richard S. Lazarus and James Deese, "The Effects of Psychological Stress upon Performance," *Psychological Bulletin,* XLIX:4, Part 1 (July 1952), 293–317.

Ulrich [19] studied emotional-stress effects on two groups of college girls, one experienced and the other inexperienced in varsity type sports. The stress situations were anticipations of different types of experience. For the experienced group, they were anticipated participation in (1) a class basketball game, (2) an intramural game, (3) an interschool game, (4) a written test in one of their regular courses, and (5) attendance at a game of some importance to them. Then one-half of each group participated in the anticipated event and the other half was denied participation. However, the anticipated and actual *interschool* experience was omitted as a stressor for the inexperienced group.

Ulrich used changes in pulse and respiration rates, and eosinophil count as her measures of degrees of stress. She reported that the inexperienced group had greater stress scores than the experienced in all situations involving basketball; that the experienced group revealed stress scores significant at the 1 per cent level only in the anticipated test and the anticipated interschool contest situations, with higher stress scores being recorded in the former. For the inexperienced group, the differential levels of stress, significant at the 1 per cent level, were in descending order: anticipation of written test, of intramural contest, and of class contest. For the post-stressor situation (after participation or denial of participation), the experienced group which was not permitted to participate registered higher stress scores than those who participated. For the inexperienced group, the reverse was true; *i.e.,* those who did participate registered higher stress scores than those who were not permitted to participate. Ulrich hypothesizes that the threshold of stress may be raised by experience in the stressor situation.

strength of motivational stress

This problem is interrelated with the change of threshold with experience. In general, the effects of an increase in stimulus show a steady rise up to a certain maximum level, different for each individual, then a drop-off, and finally a complete disruption of intelligent adaptive action.

Birch [20] studied the effects of the variation in the strength of the stimulus on ability of chimpanzees to solve a motor problem in order to get food. The lengths of food deprivation were 2, 6, 12, 24, 36, and 48 hours. Birch reported poor results with low levels and high levels of strength of motivation. When the motivation was low, the animals were easily distracted and tended to deviate into non-goal-directed behavior. Under intense motivation, the animals concentrated on the goal but shut out features of the situation which were essential to success. Those animals working under intermediate conditions of motivational intensity were more successful. Their behavior was goal directed but adequately flexible to permit solution of the problem.

---

[19] Celeste Ulrich, "Measurement of Stress Evidenced by College Women in Situations Involving Competition, *Research Quarterly,* XXVIII:2 (May 1957), 160–72.

[20] Herbert G. Birch, "The Role of Motivational Factors in Insightful Problem-Solving," *Journal of Comparative Psychology,* XXXVIII (1945), 295–317.

Mitchem and Tuttle [21] studied the effects on static neuromuscular tremor magnitude of: (1) graded bouts of exercise of differing strenuousness, (2) students' anticipation of a final written examination, and (3) wide age differences. They reported that neuromuscular tremor magnitude varied directly with the strenuousness of the exercise. They also reported that anticipation of the examination increased tremor, and that tremor was greater after sixty years than it was in adolescence.

comparison of various motivating conditions

Chase,[22] after experimenting with incentives for children of ages two to eight years, reported that praise was more effective than no motivation but that reward was more effective than praise. Leuba,[23] experimenting with fifth grade children, found little effect from praise, and got best results from a combination of rivalry, praise, a chocolate bar, and social recognition. Abel,[24] working with fifth and sixth grade boys, reported that praise was superior to no motivation but that a reward one cent per trial was superior to praise. (This was over thirty years ago when a penny would buy something for a child.) She also reported that praise seemed to lose its effectiveness as an incentive over a period of time.

Forlano [25] tested the effect of various motivating conditions on the performance of sixth grade pupils in a cancellation test. His conditions were: (1) individual improvement goal, (2) class improvement goal, (3) team improvement (class competing with class), and (4) team improvement (boys competing against girls). He reported significant superiority over base trials in two of the situations; namely, self-improvement and team improvement with boys competing against girls. Note that in the Birger Johnson study cited earlier, the junior high school boys actually did less well under competitive stress. Note also the similarity of Forlano's strongest motivating factors to those noted by Strong in the next section.

Hartrick [26] studied the effects of self-competition, reward, audience, and a nonmotivated situation on work output on a bicycle ergometer. He found significant increase in work output under the motivating situations but no significant group differences in the effects of the respective motivating conditions. He used male college undergraduates as subjects.

---

[21] John C. Mitchem and W. W. Tuttle, "Influence of Exercises, Emotional Stress, and Age on Static Neuromuscular Tremor Magnitude," *Research Quarterly,* XXV:1 (March 1954), 65–74.

[22] Lucille Chase, "Motivation of Young Children," *The University of Iowa Studies in Child Welfare,* V:3 (March 15, 1932), 9–119.

[23] Clarence J. Leuba, "A Preliminary Experiment to Qualify an Incentive and Its Effects," *Journal of Abnormal and Social Psychology,* XXV:3 (October-December 1930), 275–88.

[24] Lorraine B. Abel, "The Effects of Shifts in Motivation Upon the Learning of a Sensori-Motor Task," *Archives of Psychology,* XXIX:No. 205 (June 1936), 1–57.

[25] George Forlano, "An Experiment in Cooperation," *Journal of Educational Research,* XXV:2 (February 1932), 128–31.

[26] Frederick John Hartrick, "The Effects of Various Incentives on Performance in an Endurance Exercise" (unpublished Master of Science thesis, The Pennsylvania State University, 1960).

effect on measures of strength and physical fitness

Ryan [27] tested the effects of three different incentives on hand dynamometer scores of four groups (including a control group) of male university students. The incentives he used were: (1) verbal encouragement, (2) knowledge of past results plus sight of scoring dial while performing, (3) threat and application of electric shock for failing to improve on each trial. The control group was merely told to make a maximum effort. Ryan reported finding no significant difference among the four groups under the respective conditions. He suggests that if the subjects understand that maximum effort is to be exerted in strength testing, no additional incentive is necessary.

Strong [28] studied the relation of motivation to performance on physical performance tests. He used 434 boys and girls from the sixth grade. His experiment included both experimental and control groups and six "motivating methods." The six were: (1) competition with classmate of equal ability; (2) competition with one's own record in an attempt to improve; (3) equal group (team) competition; (4) competition within classes to set class record; (5) competition with classmate of markedly different ability; (6) level of aspiration—*i.e.*, with knowledge of his past record, the subject was urged to set a new goal, then encouraged to reach it. Strong concluded that the validity of the measures of "physical fitness tests" is dependent on the motivating conditions under which they are administered. He found that level of aspiration and team competition were the most effective of the six motivating conditions, and that the types of motivation used were more effective with boys than with girls in performance on fitness tests.

success and failure, praise and reproof, encouragement and discouragement

Laird [29] reported that when intense and personal "razzing" was given to college men taking a series of motor tests, their steadiness diminished but fatigue also diminished.

Bayton and Conley,[30] in a study of effects of success and failure stress on a manipulation task, reported that the failure stimulus was very effective after initial success, but produced inferior performance after initial failure; *i.e.*, previous success or failure determine the nature of the later response to failure.

Ulrich and Burke [31] found no difference in work output on a bicycle

---

27 E. Dean Ryan, "Effect of Differential Motive-Incentive Conditions on Physical Performance," *Research Quarterly*, XXXII:1, Part 1 (March 1961), 83–87.

28 Clinton H. Strong, "Motivation Related to Performance of Physical Fitness Tests," *Research Quarterly*, XXXIV:4 (December 1963), 497–507.

29 Donald Laird, "Changes in Motor Control and Individual Variations Under the Influence of 'Razzing,' " *Journal of Experimental Psychology*, VI (1923), 236–46.

30 James A. Bayton and Harold W. Conley, "Duration of Success Background and the Effect of Failure Upon Performance," *Journal of General Psychology*, LVI: Second Half (April 1957), 179–85.

31 Celeste Ulrich and Roger K. Burke, "Effect of Motivational Stress upon Physical Performance," *Research Quarterly*, XXVIII:4 (December 1957), 403–12.

ergometer under success and failure stressors, although these scores were significantly higher (1 per cent level and 5 per cent level, respectively) than the earlier "base" trials. However, the physiological measures indicated more expenditure of energy under failure stress.

Sparks [32] experimented with adolescent boys in the learning of an overhand volleyball serve for a three-week training period. He used a praised group, a praised and criticized group, a criticized group, and a control group. Sparks reported no significant difference in group scores measured at termination of training but significant differences in later retention. All three "motivated" groups did better than the control group. The "praise and criticism" group did better on these retention tests than any of the other groups. The praised group did not differ significantly from the criticized group.

Gates and Rissland [33] used college students in a three-hole motor co-ordination test and a color-naming test, with encouragement and discouragement as the respective motivating conditions. They concluded that some comment was better than none, and that the poor performer was more likely to be unfavorably affected by discouragement and reproof than the more proficient one.

Gilchrist [34] had his college students repeat an English examination with one-half praised for their success on the first test and the other half reproved for doing so poorly. The two groups were actually equal. On the second trial, the praised group showed a very significant improvement but the reproved group did no better, and in some cases worse, than on the first trial.

electric shock

Johanson [35] reported from an experiment that when the subjects were informed of previous reaction time immediately before a trial, simple reaction time was reduced about 6 per cent; but a mild shock administered when the reaction time was slow was more than twice as effective in reducing reaction time.

Bunch [36] reported that subjects learning a maze under the threat of electric shock learned with 50 per cent fewer trials than the control group, 30 per cent fewer errors, and in 30 per cent less time. Average time per trial indicated, however, that the subjects receiving shock responded more cautiously.

---

[32] Jack L. Sparks, "Relative Effects of Various Verbal Incentives on Learning and Retention of a Gross Motor Skill" (unpublished Master of Science thesis, The Pennsylvania State University, 1963).

[33] Georgina Gates and Louise Rissland, "The Effect of Encouragement and of Discouragement upon Performance," *Journal of Educational Psychology,* XIV:1 (January 1923), 21–26.

[34] Edward P. Gilchrist, "The Extent to Which Praise and Reproof Affect a Pupil's Work," *School and Society,* IV:101 (December 2, 1916), 872–74.

[35] Albert M. Johanson, "The Influence of Incentive and Punishment Upon Reaction Time," *Archives of Psychology,* VIII (May 1922), No. 54, pp. 1–53.

[36] Marion E. Bunch, "The Effect of Electric Shock as Punishment for Errors in Human Maze Learning," *Journal of Comparative Psychology,* VIII:4 (October 1928), 343–59.

Henry [37] found that motivating the subjects with electric shock whenever reaction or movement time was slower than the subject's average had a significant effect on speeding up the reaction or movement. Howell [38] reported that the tension caused by the use of electric shock produced an improvement in total time of motor response. Munro [39] used electric shock to motivate subjects when their speed of movement was slow. This motivation speeded up their movement time and the amount of improvement transferred to a second movement pattern; the improvement persisted for several weeks.

time-limit pressure and anxiety

Craig [40] experimented with achievement in a perceptual-motor task under two conditions—normal reaction and action forced within a limited time. Generally, higher mean scores were achieved under the time-limit situation. The conclusion is that time-limit pressure arouses a state of anxiety.

Matarazzo *et al.*[41] conducted a study to investigate the hypothesis that anxiety, as an acquired drive, would facilitate learning up to a point, but beyond this level increased anxiety would hinder learning. They used the Taylor Manifest Anxiety Scale and classified subjects into four groups on a scale of increasing anxiety level. The four groups then were put through a maze learning experience. The time required to learn by the respective groups supported their hypothesis.

personality index scores and learning or performance

The above study by Matarazzo *et al.* is really concerned with an acquired personality trait, and whether or not the effect of the motivational stressor changes with the particular aspect of personality. In the study by Sparks [42] mentioned earlier, no relationship was found between scores on the California Personality Index and rate of learning or retention while subjected to various motivational devices. France [43] found no relationship between scores on the Minnesota Multiphasic Personality Inventory and physical performance scores in three events, the hop-step-and-jump, the agility run, and pull-ups.

---

[37] Franklin M. Henry, "Increase in Speed of Movement by Motivation and by Transfer of Motivated Improvement," *Research Quarterly,* XXII:2 (May 1951), 219–28.

[38] Maxwell L. Howell, "Influence of Emotional Tension on Speed of Reaction and Movement," *Research Quarterly,* XXIV:1 (March 1953), 22–32.

[39] Sanford J. Munro, "The Retention of the Increase in Speed of Movement Transferred from a Motivated Simpler Response," *Research Quarterly,* XXII:2 (May 1951), 229–33.

[40] Eugene A. Craig, "Perceptual-Motor Task Achievement Under Two Conditions of Stimulus Display," *Journal of General Psychology,* LIII: Second Half (October 1955), 281–85.

[41] Joseph D. Matarazzo, George A. Ulett, and George Saslow, "Human Maze Performance as a Function of Increasing Levels of Anxiety," *Journal of General Psychology,* LIII: First Half (July 1955), 79–93.

[42] Sparks, *op. cit.*

[43] Wellman L. France, "A Study of Relationships between Tests of Physical Performance and Varied Traits of Personality" (unpublished doctoral thesis, Purdue University, 1953).

Walters [44] made an analysis of changes in social adjustment of "motivated" and "nonmotivated" groups during a seven-week bowling course. Her social adjustment measure was the Cowell Personal Distance Ballot. Both groups improved in social adjustment over the seven weeks, but the "motivated" group improved significantly more than the "nonmotivated" group. The writer is of the opinion that the term "nonmotivated" is a little strong for a group of bowlers who are improving and who received "the usual commendation of exceptional skill or good progress." However, this is a minor point in a study which demonstrates the value of stronger motivation in developing this greater degree of social adjustment. The individuals in the "motivated" group were provided with several additional incentive conditions, such as remaining on the same team, having scores posted, receiving publicity as team winners, and having the losers treat the winners.

an audience

Gates [45] reported a stimulating effect on performance of verbal and manual tasks when an audience was present for the group, but no improvement occurred for the better subjects in the group. Hartrick,[46] mentioned earlier, found improved performance over the control situation when an audience witnessed the performance on the bicycle ergometer. Travis [47] reported that over 80 per cent of his subjects did better on an eye-hand coordination task with a small audience present, but the group differences did not reach significance.

Empirical evidence indicates that background of the individual, general anxiety level, ego-involvement, and previous experience of success or failure have much to do with the effects of an audience on performance. The beginner may stammer or forget his lines from stage fright but the experienced actor is inspired to superb performance by a large and interested audience. The first few times the athlete plays before a large crowd are likely to be moments of high emotional tension. With reasonable success, he finds less difficulty in appearing subsequently and in directing this energy from emotional stress into effective action. However, if he makes serious errors and is severely criticized on his first appearances, his level of anxiety may become too high to permit rapid and adequate adjustments on succeeding appearances. Let us examine a few studies of emotional stress in athletes.

emotional reactions of athletes

Warren Johnson [48] completed a study of emotional reactions at the University of Denver. He used observation and interview plus measures of

[44] C. Etta Walters, "A Sociometric Study of Motivated and Non-Motivated Bowling Groups," *Research Quarterly,* XXVI:1 (March 1955), 107–12.

[45] Georgina Gates, "The Effect of an Audience upon Performance," *Journal of Abnormal and Social Psychology,* XVIII:4 (January-March 1924), 334–44.

[46] Hartrick, *op. cit.*

[47] Lee E. Travis, "The Effect of a Small Audience upon Eye-Hand Coordination," *Journal of Abnormal and Social Psychology,* XX:2 (July 1925), 142–46.

[48] Warren R. Johnson, "A Study of Emotion Revealed in Two Types of Athletic Contests," *Research Quarterly,* XX:1 (March 1949), 72–79.

changes in heart rate, blood pressure, and blood sugar. The measures were taken (1) four to six days before the contest, (2) the day before the contest, (3) a few hours before the contest, (4) immediately before the contest, and (5) fifteen minutes after the contest. Johnson reported only mild pre-contest emotion in football players but a "very considerable" amount in wrestlers. In a later study,[49] Johnson used eighty-two winter sports athletes from New England colleges. His tools of measurement were a psychogal-vanometer to measure changes in skin resistance under emotional disturbance, and two word-association tests. He concluded in this second study that the pre-contest situation is characterized by "a tendency toward exaggerated psychogalvanic reactivity." He says:

> However, attention is called to the consideration that the "disturbed state" that so commonly characterizes the precontest situation is probably not detri-mental to individuals who are comparatively free of profound personality disturbances.[50]

He also states that "In no case did men who were considered outstanding performers by their coaches react in an extreme manner." He agrees with Magda Arnold[51] that, within limits, varieties of emotional disturbance probably serve to improve neurological and endocrine integration for com-petitive action.

Harmon and Johnson[52] reported a study of like nature, using nineteen track men in a preliminary study and forty-two experienced football players later; the latter group had an average of seven years of playing experience. The subjects were all college men, and most of the football players were war veterans. The experimenters had the coaches rate the importance of the respective games early in the season. The subjects were given a base test which was separated far enough from any contest to permit a relaxed reaction. Then each subject was tested approximately twenty-five minutes before each contest. The measures used were a galvanic skin response, systolic blood pressure, and pulse rate.

All three measures revealed pre-contest "emotional disturbance." The experimenters reported a close relationship between the amount of "emo-tional disturbance" and the coaches' rating of the relative importance of each game. The investigators also concluded that the galvanic skin response was the best single indicator, and that the "regulars" were best for pre-dicting degree of "upness."

Skubic[53] used a galvanic skin response measure to check excited state before participation of boys playing Little League and Middle League com-petitive baseball. She measured 206 boys ranging in age from nine through

---

[49] Warren R. Johnson, "Psychogalvanic and Word Association Studies of Athletes," *Research Quarterly*, XXII:4 (December 1951), 427–33.

[50] *Ibid.*, p. 432.

[51] Magda Arnold, "Physiological Differentiation of Emotional States," *Psychological Review*, LII:1 (January 1945), 35–48.

[52] John M. Harmon and Warren R. Johnson, "The Emotional Reactions of College Athletes," *Research Quarterly*, XXIII:4 (December 1952), 391–97.

[53] Elvera Skubic, "Emotional Responses of Boys to Little League and Middle League Competitive Baseball," *Research Quarterly*, XXVI:3 (October 1955), 342–52.

fifteen, and a group of eighty nonplayers of similar ages as a control group. All subjects were tested immediately before softball competition in physical education class, immediately after the class, and one-and-one-half hours after the class. Then the Little League and Middle League team players were tested immediately before competition in baseball, immediately after the game was over, and again one-and-one-half hours after the game. This procedure was repeated for three games. All subjects, both players and non-players, were also tested at other times when they were "in the most relaxed state possible."

Skubic reported that, in general, the players at all ages showed less change from the resting level than the nonplayers at all ages; that the players tended to show less emotionality than the nonplayers; and that league competition produced no more emotional reaction (as indicated by the galvanic skin response) than physical education class games in softball. Skubic cautions the reader not to take the galvanic skin response measure as necessarily a presentation of the whole picture of emotional response. Her findings agree with other studies in indicating that experience with stress tends to raise the threshold of stress.

SUMMARY

Motivation is a state of being aroused to action. This arousal may result from organic needs such as hunger or thirst, or from psychic needs such as the need for association with one's fellows, for affiliation and affection, or to explore and manipulate one's environment. Many needs are conditioned and directed through learning into secondary or derived motives, such as pride in one's work or in one's appearance, drive to complete a job once started, or drive to perfect one's skill in music, art, or sport.

Some degree of motivational arousal is essential for significant learning. When possible, intrinsic motivation, a desire just to learn and be able to perform the task, is the most desirable type of motivation. This type occurs when the adolescent wants to learn to drive a car or to skate, for example. It can occur in many situations. To take an extreme example, it can occur in foreign language learning if the youngster wants to communicate with his associates when he is of necessity living in a foreign country as a result of foreign service assignment of his father. However, intrinsic motivation is often not possible, especially when the student is first introduced to the new activity; hence the need for extra incentives. Incentives are external stimuli used to get people to do tasks irrespective of any satisfaction inherent in the doing of the task itself. Rewards, grades, bonuses, and special recognitions are types of incentives. The type of motivational stimulus that will have the desired effect and the degree to which it should be used are problems of individual diagnosis and prescription by the teacher.

Emotion is sometimes defined as a deep psychic disturbance and a generalized upset of homeostasis; but for our purposes in this chapter, we have defined emotion as: *the conscious feeling tone* which accompanies degrees of motivation high enough to stimulate an excess of energy release, certain generalized reactions such as activity of the sympathetic division of the autonomic nervous system, visceral and glandular reactions, and the chemical and physiological changes thereby initiated. We have limited the definition of emotional expression to include only certain learned patterns of stimulus situations and responses, psychic in nature and characterized by great depths of feeling. We use the word "certain" to exclude upsets caused by illnesses or physical injuries, except insofar as they also stimulate fear, anxiety, or anger.

The effects of motivation on learning and performance are best represented by a climb up and over the brow of a hill to the sudden drop-off of a cliff; *i.e.*, improvement increases up to the individual's adjustment tolerance level, then declines until, farther along on the continuum, there is a complete lack of adaptive behavior. The amount of motivation which is effective varies with the individual, his background and experience, his level of learning in the stimulating situation, and his preceding experience of success or failure in the particular situation.

Stress is a term used to represent efforts of the body to recover from a generalized upset or imbalance in its normal equilibrium or homeostasis. The upset of homeostasis may be caused by strong physical effort, strong psychic stimuli, toxic poisons, disease, or tissue injury. The term is generally used to describe the defense-reaction efforts of the body when it is seriously upset and imbalanced by stimuli strong enough to cause somewhat generalized visceral and glandular activity. Emotional-arousal situations are only one type of the many stress-producing situations.

Praise and criticism, encouragement and discouragement, rewards and punishment, and ego-involvement (self-respect, status, prestige) are devices used to stimulate learning and/or performance. Previous denial of a need or desire, denial of recognition or praise for example, strengthen the later effect of recognition or praise as an incentive. With much praise, however, the motivating effectiveness of it disappears. This principle of satiation applies to many incentives and drives. Reproof and punishment for maladapted action or error can be effective if they are not too strong or too frequent, and if they are followed by praise or reward for adjusted action. Competition and rivalry have strong arousal effects but the results vary with the individual, his age, level of learning, previous experience of success or failure, and the presence of an interested audience. Thresholds of specific motivational stimuli seem to rise with experience; *i.e.*, one learns to perform effectively under stimuli whose strength would have been disruptive earlier in the learning stage.

Athletes experience what is called emotional arousal before important contests, much as most students experience similar feelings with accompanying physiological changes before an important course examination. Unless it reaches an extreme degree, this additional stimulation tends to be beneficial rather than disruptive to the experienced person.

discussion questions

1. Is the urge to play an acquired motive?
2. Is man naturally lazy?
3. Are the needs for affection and for affiliation with one's own kind learned motives?
4. Does a mild degree of emotion tend to improve performance?
5. Does the degree of emotional stimulus which can be tolerated without interference with performance depend on the level of learning of the tasks being performed?
6. Are there *qualitative* changes in physiological functioning which accompany strong emotional stimulus?
7. Did William James think that emotion was the physiological change caused by strong stimuli?
8. Does the field of psychosomatic medicine indicate that physiological changes may result from mental states? Vice versa?
9. Is stress limited to bodily defense reactions to *overstimulus?*
10. Does Hellebrandt seem to think that extreme stress is occasionally productive of much faster learning or better performance?
11. Is there an apparent desire for emotional overtones by the normal human being during his everyday life?
12. Is competition an almost universal characteristic of human behavior?
13. Does the effect of praise on learning tend to diminish if it is continued over a considerable span of time?
14. Does the threshold of emotional stress tend to rise with experience in situations which cause stress? Is this change in threshold specific to the particular stressful situation?
15. Girls seem to be less highly motivated than boys by the typical incentives used in fitness tests. Is this due to a difference in value concepts of the two sexes?
16. May the effectiveness of electric shock in accelerating certain types of learning merely be due to the stronger and more precise feedback of information as to results of action?
17. Does learning tend to cease completely when the emotional stimulus becomes excessively strong?
18. Evidence indicates that there is much emotion accompanying athletic competition. Generally speaking, does this emotional factor tend to cause less effective performance?

DEFINE:

Motivation
Emotion
Stress
Incentive

VIII

Measurement and
Prediction of
Learning and Performance

It is necessary, first, to make clear to the reader just what we are trying to measure before we can discuss methods of measurement. The term learning will be used in this chapter to mean improvement—both rate of improvement and amount of improvement. It has either no correlation or a negative correlation with initial skill. Initial skill represents the stage at which the individual has arrived as a result of aptitude for learning plus past practice and experience. Because of the wide variation in interest and experience among individuals, one cannot judge individual learning aptitude by observing initial level of skill; nor can one judge learning aptitude by *change* in gross score on skill tests. Improvement in performance is more difficult at higher levels, so that interpretation of improvement in terms of raw-score changes at various levels would make the individual starting at the higher level seem to be a slower learner, for his amount of change in performance would be numerically less. Moreover, the individual's performance at any one time may be affected by such factors as motivation, fatigue, or physiological fluctuations.

Performance is different from learning. It is the skill level as it functions at any one time. Learning is an interpretation of improvements in performance as estimated from successive performance measures over a span of time. If we wish to compare individuals in their relative improvement on the same learning task, we must make sure that they have the same amounts of practice, equal motivation, like procedures, and that the scores represent results after comparable amounts of practice which are interpretable in terms of the same units of difficulty in the learning process.

THE MEASUREMENT OF LEARNING
AT VARIOUS LEVELS

1. per cent gain of initial score

One of the ways used extensively in the past to measure improvement (learning) was to measure the initial performance, or perhaps the average of the first two or three trials, then compute the learning from following practices in terms of per cent of improvement over the initial score. McCraw gives a good example of the fallacy in this method of computing learning. He compares an improvement in the broad jump from 8 to 10 feet, with an improvement from 20 to 22 feet. The first ratio of improvement to initial score ($\frac{2}{8}$) indicates 25 per cent improvement, whereas the second ratio ($\frac{2}{20}$) indicates only 10 per cent improvement. Yet, in relative difficulty, the second change would seem to be much harder to attain than the first.

2. lack of equivalency of numerical units

Failure to recognize the difference in difficulty at different levels in the measurement of learning occurs when teachers grade in terms of progress scores, regardless of the initial level of the learner. Those who start at the lower levels have much less difficulty in demonstrating progress. The basic principle proposed by McCraw which many other experimenters in the field stress is that numerical gains after high initial scores should have more value than the same numerical gains after low or moderate initial scores.

Counting the numerical change as equal at these different ability levels gives a distorted picture of learning. The change from 12 seconds to 11.8 seconds in the 100-yard dash surely does not represent the same amount of improvement as the change from 10 seconds to 9.8 seconds; or the change in a bowling score from 80 to 120 does not represent as much improvement as the change from 160 to 200.

When numerical progress is used as the measure of learning and of grading and rewarding, some individuals, knowing they must show "progress," learn not to score high on the initial tests. It is much easier to improve from a low initial score than from a high one. Actually, the relationship of the initial score both to the amount and the rate of improvement (in terms of raw-score change) ranges from a very low to a negative correlation in most learning studies.

3. methods of computing individual improvement

Let us assume that valid measures of learning will take into account the increase in difficulty as one progresses toward his maximum, that numerical increments are decreasing as the individual approaches his limit, and that the method of measurement of improvement will in some way adjust the inequality due to different initial stages. A simple example of one method of computing per cent of improvement or learning rate follows:

learning score per session $= \dfrac{\text{amount of change per session}}{\text{maximum score minus score at end of preceding practice}}$

If the task is to shoot 100 free throws, the maximum is 100. If, in the preceding session, the subject was successful 45 times out of 100 and is successful 55 tries out of 100 in the current session, the above formula becomes: $\dfrac{55-45}{100-45}$ or 18 per cent improvement. Now suppose he averages 63 out of 100 the next practice session. We then have $\dfrac{63-55}{100-55}$ or $\dfrac{8}{45}$, 17.8 per cent. In other words, although he improved only eight more successful tries (two less than his improvement in the preceding practice), he was still maintaining approximately the same rate of improvement. An example from nearer the maximum might make this point clearer. Suppose he completed 85 tries out of 100 successfully on his preceding practice and completes 88 successfully in the current practice. The per cent becomes:

$$\frac{88-85}{100-85} \text{ or } \frac{3}{15} \text{ or } 20 \text{ per cent.}$$

Of course the problem is not this simple. There are too many fluctuations due to uncontrollable factors to permit an increase with each practice which is a constant per cent of what is left to learn. Several successive practices would perhaps have to be averaged—perhaps scores for a week of practice in such a skill as the free-throw of basketball, in order to smooth out the gross fluctuations. Moreover, the individual's own limit or asymptote is very likely to be somewhere below perfection, the world's record, or whatever criterion one uses for the limit of what is left to learn.

The perfect maximum may be far beyond the capabilities of all but a fraction of 1 per cent of the subjects. It is doubtful if the average person would reach a limit beyond 85 out of 100 in the above example. If we compute his improvement on the basis of 100 instead of 85, we are introducing an error into our formula; *i.e.,* we are computing his "per cent of learning of what is left to learn before he reaches his limit" with a denominator far beyond his capacity to learn. His computed score on rate of improvement, instead of remaining relatively constant, will be too low, especially in the last quartile or more of his learning sessions. We can compute the individual's improvement using the average plateau score of previous groups as our best approximation of his limit. If his rate of improvement does not equal the group average in spite of like conditions of practice and motivation, we then assume he has less specific ability to learn this skill, a lower final maximum, or both.

The truth is we cannot do a precise calculation and analysis of a subject's learning until he has reached his individual plateau and we have all his practice scores available. We do know that each individual will have a unique learning curve and that this curve will change if the learning task is changed; in other words, there is individual difference in learning aptitude and the amount of this difference is specific to the learning task.

For adequate estimation, one needs the raw scores of the learning of a great number of subjects in the specific skill. Then one can compute an average per cent of improvement per practice in terms of the average limit reached by the large group. A comparison of an individual's progress with the large sample will show whether he is above or below average in improvement rate. Of course such group improvement rates would only be applicable to the one skill from which the scores were taken. With change of skill, both individual and group rates would change.

In summary, a valid measure of learning should represent the amount of improvement occurring under the same conditions and lengths of practice; *i.e.*, at the higher and more complex levels where learning is more difficult, the amount of practice time necessary to make the change must be taken into account in the measurement of learning. This principle is the reason we have advocated that the computation of *improvement be in proportion to what is yet to be learned before the limit is reached*. Bachman, in reviewing the experimental studies in this area, says:

> It may reasonably be postulated that learning should taper off with increased practice, approaching a performance plateau, and that the amount of improvement caused by a stated amount of practice (for example, one trial at any point on the curve) should be a constant proportion of the amount still to be learned, this amount being defined as the difference between the skill or performance at that particular trial and the skill at the plateau. In other words, improvement should become relatively more difficult as the plateau is approached.[1]

STUDIES OF IMPROVEMENT COMPUTATION

McCraw,[2] in an extensive study of methods of scoring tests of motor learning, says that the method of "Per Cent Gain of Initial Score" appears to be wholly invalid; that the methods of (1) adding the scores of all trials in the learning tests including the initial and final scores ("The Total Learning Score" method), and (2) "Per Cent Gain of Possible Gain" are the most valid methods to use when trying to compare individuals with different initial scores. He suggests that warm-up trials at the start not be counted as practice trials, nor should initial scores if they deviate greatly. However, one should be careful not to exclude so many of these first trials that the trials used as the measure of initial score will include improvement. He also calls attention to the fact that many individuals achieve maximum efficiency before final trials, and that this maximum performance should be considered in computations of "per cent gain of possible gain."

---

[1] John C. Bachman, "Motor Learning and Performance as Related to Age and Sex in Two Measures of Balance Coordination," *Research Quarterly*, XXXII:2 (May 1961), 124.

[2] L. W. McCraw, "Comparative Analysis of Methods of Scoring Tests of Motor Learning," *Research Quarterly*, XXVI:4 (December 1955), 440–53.

Henry [3] reports a study of the problem of evaluating motor learning when the performance levels are heterogeneous—*i.e.,* when the initial scores of subjects vary widely. He evaluated the respective learning scores of his subjects in three motor skills: vertical jumping, a fast arm-movement task, and a balancing task. He found negative correlations (−.60; −.68; −.73) between initial performance raw scores and amount of raw score improvement in all three learning tasks. Although the poorest showed the most improvement in the raw scores, they still scored poorly in final skill. Henry says, therefore, that it would illogical to consider their motor educability as high. The raw learning scores were unrelated to final degree of skill. Henry proposes a formula for computing derived learning scores which is designed to hold constant the influence of initial skill. He says that, by the use of this formula, the corrected scores on the three learning tasks are found to be unrelated to initial skill but substantially correlated with raw learning scores and also with final skill attainment.[4]

"MOTOR EDUCABILITY TESTS"

There are in the literature various "motor educability tests" which purport to measure the individual's aptitude for motor learning, thereby enabling one to predict his approximate degree of success in learning a new skill. The present stage of investigation indicates that these so-called educability tests do not measure motor learning aptitude or predict relative progress in learning. Gire and Espenschade [5] compared the scores on three of these educability tests with the achievement and learning of basketball, volleyball, and baseball skills during a semester of instruction (eight weeks of basketball, three weeks of volleyball, and five weeks of baseball). The investigators correlated their skill-test scores in the three sports with three motor educability tests—the Brace Scale of Motor Ability, the Iowa Revision of the Brace Test, and the Johnson Physical Skill Tests for Sectioning Classes into Homogeneous Groups. The investigators say:

> All correlations are very low and in most cases not significant. Negative relationships are the rule in the correlations of all "educability" tests with the criterion of "motor" learning. These negative relationships indicate that those

---

[3] Franklin M. Henry, "Evaluation of Motor Learning When Performance Levels Are Heterogeneous," *Research Quarterly,* XXVII:2 (May 1956), 176–81.

[4] Henry uses the method of residuals to hold statistically constant the influence of initial skill. His formula is: $W = Y - bX + C$ where W is the attainment score, Y is the individual's learning score, C is bM_x and b is $r_{xy} \frac{\sigma_y}{\sigma_x}$. Note that r_{xy} is usually negative. In addition to the article by Franklin M. Henry already cited, see two other articles by him: "Condition Ratings and Endurance Measures," *Research Quarterly,* XX:2 (May 1949), 126–133; and "Errors in Measurement," in *Research Methods Applied to Health, Physical Education and Recreation* (Washington, D.C.: The American Association for Health, Physical Education, and Recreation, 1949), p. 463.

[5] Eugenia Gire and Anna Espenschade, "The Relationship Between Measures of Motor Educability and the Learning of Specific Motor Skills," *Research Quarterly,* XIII:1 (March 1942), 43–56.

individuals who are the best early in the season make the least progress; *i.e.*, achieve less. . . . The degree of relationship in all cases is too low to obtain reliable prediction of any one criterion.[6]

The investigators conclude that

. . . no test of "motor educability" studied measured accurately the ease with which the subjects in this study learned new skills or relearned old ones in basketball, volleyball, and baseball in regular physical education classes.[7]

Brace [8] reported a series of studies at the University of Texas in which scores on the Brace Motor Ability and the Iowa-Brace Motor Ability Tests were compared with scores of 275 high school girls learning five motor activities. The number of trials needed to perform perfectly was taken as the score for each activity. The activities were: (1) a dance step to be performed correctly to count; (2) scoring twelve points with three balls in driving a hockey ball at a target; (3) bouncing a tennis ball on a racket ten consecutive times while standing in a three-foot circle; (4) executing a headstand and a handstand for ten seconds, in any form; and (5) bouncing a volleyball against a wall with both hands six times in succession. Brace states:

Conclusions from the data would seem to indicate that either the so-called learning tests do not measure ability to learn or that the other measures obtained have little relationship to ability to learn motor skills.[9]

In the same article, Brace reports a learning study in swimming, using eighty-nine girls from grades six, seven, and eight, all beginning swimmers. The number of trials needed by each girl to pass ten swimming-type tests was correlated with scores on the Brace and Iowa-Brace Tests. Brace says: ". . . the data indicate that neither of these tests has predictive value, and no proof has been produced that these tests are tests of motor educability."

Gross, Griesel, and Stull [10] conducted a study of various measures of learning in a wrestling class of fifty-six college students, none of whom had ever had any wrestling experience before. The subjects were given the Iowa Revision of the Brace Test, and the Metheny Revision of the Johnson Test during the first week of the course. The investigators reported a correlation of only .40 between the scores on these two tests. Ratings of progress and achievement were made by the instructors, who had watched them during the course in class competition bouts, and by outside experts in wrestling, who evaluated them at the last part of the course. The correlation between the Iowa-Brace test scores and the combined rating on wrestling was .46;

---

[6] *Ibid.*, p. 53.

[7] *Ibid.*

[8] D. K. Brace, "Studies in the Rate of Learning Gross Bodily Motor Skills," *Research Quarterly*, XII:2 (May 1941), 181–85.

[9] *Ibid.*, p. 182.

[10] E. A. Gross, Donald C. Griesel, and Alan Stull, "Relationship Between Two Motor Educability Tests, a Strength Test, and Wrestling Ability After Eight-Weeks' Instruction," *Research Quarterly*, XXVII:4 (December 1956), 395–402.

and between the Metheny Revision of the Johnson test and the wrestling rating, .33.

Various tests have been devised which purported to measure "general motor ability" or to predict future performance of individuals in various fine and gross motor activities. Authorities are not in agreement as to the abilities which are described as *general traits of the individual,* as con-contrasted with specific abilities. Fleishman [11] has emphasized motor abilities ("more general traits of the individual which have been inferred from certain response consistencies") as well as specific skills. Henry, on the other hand, tends to emphasize the specific nature of motor learning. He says:

> The theory of specific motor abilities implies that some individuals are gifted with many specific abilities and others with only a few; it follows that there will inevitably be significant correlations between total test battery scores when tests involving many abilities are lumped together. The general motor factor which thus makes its appearance is a sample, fundamentally, of how many specifics the individual has, and general motor ability does exist in this sense.[12]

Most of the so-called general motor ability batteries seem to have about the same predictive value as the "motor educability" batteries discussed above. For historical reasons, one such battery, developed outside the physical education field, will be discussed briefly below.

THE STANFORD MOTOR SKILLS UNIT [13]

The Stanford Motor Skills Unit is a battery of motor tasks designed to predict an individual's performance on various types of manual motor skills. The battery is made up of the six tasks listed below:

Spool packing—speed of bimanual coordination.
Koerth Pursuit Rotor—accuracy in following a moving target.
Motor rhythmic—precision in repeating an auditory rhythm on a tapping key.
Serial discrimination—quickness in making discriminatory finger responses to number signals.
Tapping speed—measured on a telegraph key.
Speed rotor—speed of arm, wrist, and finger movements in turning a hand drill.

Three studies will be cited relative to its effectiveness in prediction.

Walker and Adams [14] used the Stanford Motor Skills Unit in an experiment in which they tried to predict typing progress and achievement. They used

[11] E. A. Fleishman, *The Structure and Measurement of Physical Fitness* (Englewood Cliffs, N.J.: Prentice-Hall, Inc., 1964), Chap. 2; "An Analysis of Positioning Movements and Static Reactions," *Journal of Experimental Psychology,* LV:1 (January 1958), 13.

[12] Franklin M. Henry, "Specificity vs. Generality in Learning Motor Skills," *Proceedings of College Physical Education Association,* LXI (1958), 127.

[13] R. H. Seashore, "Stanford Motor Skills Unit," *Psychological Monographs,* XXXIX (1929), 51–56.

[14] Robert Walker and Raymond Adams, "Motor Skill: The Validity of Serial Motor Tests for Predicting Typewriting Proficiency," *Journal of General Psychology,* XI (July 1934), 173–86.

seventy male students, ranging in age from fifteen to seventeen years. The subjects were first tested on the Stanford Motor Skills Unit, then trained in typing for seven months. They were then tested with two typing tests. The investigators reported finding no significant relationship between the Stanford Motor Skills Unit scores and the typing scores.

Sigfrid Seashore [15] conducted an extensive study of prediction with the Stanford Motor Skills Unit in the Jantzen Knitting Mills in Portland, Oregon. He administered the Skills Unit to fifty employees in an attempt to predict their proficiency in operating a knitting machine. The scores on the machines were in terms of amount of work done and amount of yarn used. The men's work was scored for the first two weeks and for the last two weeks of their training period. The correlation between the scores on the Stanford Unit and on the machines was .14. Seashore then tested ten men who had been dropped from the industry because of their failure to maintain satisfactory standards of production. A comparison of the scores of these unsuccessful men with the scores of the ten most successful machine operators revealed that each group excelled in three of the tests. Seashore concluded that skills are highly individual and specific, and that many factors influence an individual's performance on motor-skill tests.

Many investigators have reported similar results with so-called "motor educability" and "motor ability" tests. For example, in a study involving methods in teaching swimming, Dillon [16] reported a correlation of −.02 between the Iowa Revision of the Brace Test and improvement in swimming speed. Stull,[17] in a study of effects of distribution of practice on the learning of swimming, found no correlation between the J.C.R. Test (Sargent jump, chin-ups, and shuttle run) and the various measures of swimming. However, the problem of measuring needs much more analysis than merely the correlating of performance scores on such tests with learning rates and achievement.

STUDIES OF TASK SPECIFICITY

There is much evidence that individuals do not have a general motor-learning ability, or a general motor-learning capacity. Not only do individuals vary greatly in learning rates under comparable conditions, but each individual varies in learning rate from activity to activity. Learning rates are specific to the individual and the individual's learning rate is specific to the task. Henry, who has been investigating this area for a number of years, says:

> . . . it is no longer possible to justify the concept of unitary abilities such as coordination and agility, since the evidence shows that these abilities are specific to the test or activity.[18]

---

[15] Sigfrid Seashore, "Aptitude Hypothesis in Motor Skills," *Journal of Experimental Psychology*, XIV (1931), 555–61.

[16] Evelyn K. Dillon, "A Study of the Use of Music as an Aid in Teaching Swimming," *Research Quarterly*, XXIII:1 (March 1952), 1–8.

[17] G. Alan Stull, "Relationship of Quantity and Distribution of Practice to Endurance, Speed, and Skill Development by Beginners" (unpublished doctoral thesis, The Pennsylvania State University, 1961).

[18] Henry, "Specificity vs. Generality in Learning Motor Sklls," p. 126.

. . . The evidence from controlled research gives no indication that there is any quantitatively important unitary function that can be called general coordination. On the contrary, it must be conceded that coordinations are highly specific—it is largely a matter of chance whether an individual who is highly coordinated in one type of performance will be well or poorly coordinated in another. This does not of course exclude the possibility of a few "natural athletes" who are so fortunate as to be gifted with a large number of specifics, or the "motor moron," that unfortunate individual who has few or none.[19]

Studies of various types of motor behavior and the intercorrelation between their measures follow. It is hoped that the sampling of such studies is extensive enough to permit the reader some tentative generalizations as to specificity of motor learning and performance.

Some thirty-seven years ago, R. H. Seashore published his much quoted study on "Individual Differences in Motor Skills." [20] He tested fifty subjects on eight fine motor skills and found that the intercorrelations averaged only .25. He stated that his findings argued against any theory of general motor ability and in favor of specific skills, and that the theory of determining motor skills by measuring a relatively small number of motor capacities was very questionable.

In 1934 Ragsdale and Breckenfield [21] tested junior high school boys in various skills from four different athletic sports. Although they intimated that certain group factors, such as strength, speed, and accuracy, might exist, they concluded, from the low intercorrelations of the different tests, that it was erroneous to speak of general motor ability.

In his doctoral thesis at Columbia University in 1935, Jones [22] reported intercorrelations of test scores of over 2,000 college men in five athletic-type tasks. The tasks were: running high jump, standing bar vault, rope climb, sprint run, and baseball throw for accuracy. His correlations were all so low as to indicate great specificity of motor ability.

Rarick [23] attempted to analyze the speed factor in simple athletic activities through factor analysis of scores of college men in: strength, vertical jumping, sprint, and shot put. He reported low correlations except for that between the sprint and the vertical jump (.63). This higher correlation between jumping and sprinting has been reported since in other studies and may indicate common elements between the jump and the strong explosive push on each stride in the sprints, for the length and rapidity of the dashman's strides indicate extensive springing action.

Harold Seashore [24] reported two studies at Springfield College, Adrian's

[19] Franklin M. Henry, "Coordination and Motor Learning," *Proceedings of College Physical Education Association,* LIX (1956), 68–69.

[20] R. H. Seashore, "Individual Differences in Motor Skills," *Journal of General Psychology,* III (1930), 38–65.

[21] C. E. Ragsdale and I. J. Breckenfield, "The Organization of Physical and Motor Traits in Junior High School Boys," *Research Quarterly,* V:3 (October 1934), 47–55.

[22] L. M. Jones, *Factorial Ability in Fundamental Motor Skills,* Contributions to Education No. 665 (New York: Columbia University Bureau of Publications, 1935).

[23] Lawrence Rarick, "An Analysis of the Speed Factor in Simple Athletic Activities," *Research Quarterly,* VIII:4 (December 1937), 89–92.

[24] Harold G. Seashore, "Some Relationships of Fine and Gross Motor Abilities," *Research Quarterly,* XIII:3 (October 1942), 259–74.

on balance and steadiness and Wollenberger's comparison of physical education majors and nonmajors. He says that Adrian's study permits the conclusion that "groups of college men of known differences in gross motor ability . . . do not differ significantly in the two types of finer coordinations measured." He concludes, in part, with respect to Wollenberger's investigation that the results furnish added evidence of a lack of relationship between fine and gross motor abilities.

Seashore then did an elaborate intercorrelational analysis of scores of a sample of 103 men who had taken a large battery of motor ability tests, including both fine and gross motor tasks. He again finds "essential independence" of fine and gross motor abilities. However, the intercorrelations among the gross motor tasks reveal the same lack of significant relationship. The average correlation between these gross tasks was .26; and only nine out of fifty-five correlations computed between the various gross motor tasks exceeded .40. The great similarity in the nature of the task seemed to explain some of these nine, such as the "r" of .69 between chinning and dips and the "r" of .53 between the vertical jump and the standing broadjump.

Scott,[25] in an attempt to establish tests for the measurement of kinesthesis, administered twenty-eight measures of kinesthesis and two of motor ability to 100 college women. In a second sample, she tested seventy college women with fifteen of the previous tests and a new test which supposedly measured kinesthetic influences in space orientation. Scott reported little interrelationship among the tests, and no evidence of a general kinesthetic capacity.

Fleishman[26] investigated differences between terminal accuracy (moving limbs to specific points) and steadiness (holding a limb steady while in a fixed position) such as are required in piloting aircraft. He reported over 200 correlations. Most of these correlations were quite low. Fleishman says, however, in a 1966 publication:

> From the patterns of correlations obtained, we have been able to account for performance on this wide range of tasks in terms of a relatively small number of abilities. In subsequent studies our definitions of these abilities and their distinctions from one another are becoming more clearly delineated.[27]

In a study on "Age Differences and Interrelationships Between Skill and Learning in Gross Motor Performance of Ten- and Fifteen-Year-Old Boys," [28] Henry and Nelson tested seventy-two boys on the learning of three sensory-motor skills. They make the following statements with respect to task specificity:

[25] M. Gladys Scott, "Measurement of Kinesthesis," *Research Quarterly,* XXVI:3 (October 1955), 324–41.

[26] Fleishman, "An Analysis of Positioning Movements and Static Reactions." *J. Exp. Psych.,* LV (1958), 13–246.

[27] E. A. Fleishman, "Human Abilities and the Acquisition of Skill," comments on the paper "Individual Differences," presented by Marshall B. Jones at a conference on Acquisition of Skill, New Orleans, March 8–12, 1966. See Edward A. Bilodeau, ed., *Acquisition of Skill* (New York: Academic Press, 1966), p. 152.

[28] Franklin M. Henry and Gaylord H. Nelson, "Age Differences and Interrelationships Between Skill and Learning in Gross Motor Performance of Ten- and Fifteen-Year-Old Boys," *Research Quarterly,* XXVII:2 (May 1956), 162–75.

None of the intertask correlations of amount of learning is significantly different from zero at the 1-per-cent level of confidence. . . .

Evidently the learning of motor tasks, at least those of the type used in this experiment, is not a matter of motor learning ability—rather, it is a matter of specific aptitudes for learning specific tasks. . . .

Even among gross tasks that are similar, task-specificity is great; it tends, however, to be less in the younger boy.[29]

Henry and Whitley [30] reported finding no significant correlation between static strength and strength in action (arm mass times speed of movement) in two experiments with college men as subjects. They state:

. . . individual differences in static strength can not predict "strength in action," in particular as it is exhibited by maximal speed of movement in a 90 degree horizontal arm swing fom the shoulder pivot. Neuromuscular control patterns are apparently specific and different when the muscle is moving a limb as compared with causing simple static tension.[31]

The results agree with the concept that strength as ordinarily measured is determined by a neuromuscular coordination pattern rather than the ultimate physiological capacity of the muscle.[32]

Lotter [33] completed a study relative to the specificity or generality of speed in systematically related movements. His subjects, eighty college men, were tested for speed of single and repetitive movements of each arm and each leg; and in speed of pedalling, first with the two hands, then with the two feet. He found very little generality—six of his "r_2" computations ranged from 2 per cent to .4 per cent. He did find 15 per cent and 17 per cent, respectively, of generality between the single-arm and single-leg pedalling task, and between the two-arm and two-leg pedalling task.

Smith [34] explored the problem of the specificity of the details of a particular motor act; *i.e.,* whether or not individual differences are specific not only to the particular limb but also to the direction of the movement and to the particular element measured (strength, speed, reaction latency). Smith reports from his findings:

Individual differences in limb action abilities (considering reaction latency, strength, and speed as the components of such action) tend to be highly specific to the component, to the limb involved in the action (arm or leg), the direction it is moved (forward or backward), the dynamic or static nature of

[29] *Ibid.,* pp. 167, 168–69, 175.

[30] Franklin M. Henry and J. D. Whitley, "Relationship Between Individual Differences in Strength, Speed, and Mass in an Arm Movement," *Research Quarterly,* XXXI:1 (March 1960), 24–33.

[31] *Ibid.,* pp. 32–33.

[32] *Ibid.,* p. 24 (in abstract).

[33] William S. Lotter, "Specificity or Generality of Speed of Systematically Related Movements," *Research Quarterly,* XXXII:1 (March 1961), 55–62.

[34] Leon E. Smith, "Individual Differences in Strength, Reaction Latency, Mass and Length of Limbs, and Their Relation to Maximal Speed of Movement," *Research Quarterly,* XXXII:2 (May 1961), 208–20.

the action (speed vs. measured strength), and the phase of the action (reaction latency vs. speed of movement). For some of the findings, cross-validation using other published data is available and lends additional support to the hypothesis.[35]

In a study of "Specificity and Generality in Learning and Performing Two Large Muscle Tasks," Bachman [36] reported "little more than zero correlation" between the individual scores of 320 subjects on the learning of two motor tasks. The tasks were balancing on a stabilometer and climbing a free-standing ladder. The correlations between the two tasks were not significant either for learning scores or for performance scores. He reported 3 per cent or less of generality in the skills.

Tyler,[37] in a study of the interrelationships of scores on various balance tests and abilities in three sports (basketball, gymnastics, and swimming), found significant though low correlations between swimming and some of his balance measures, somewhat less correlation with gymnastics, and no correlation between basketball abilities and any of his balance measures. His average "r" between the various balance tests was .26 with a range from .10 to .45.

Valentine [38] completed a study of various measures of balance and their relationship to improvement and skill in dancing and skating. She found very little correlation between her various measures of balance. These measures were a balance board, a balance stick (administered with eyes open and with eyes closed), and a balance beam. The average of her intercorrelations between the various balance measures was .29, including the "r" of .53 between the eyes-open and eyes-closed measures on the balance stick. She found significant correlations between certain of the balance measures and both skill and improvement in skating and *advanced* dance.

Reeves [39] administered seven different types of balance tests to a group of eighty-three college men in a study of balance as related to swimming. As part of his study, he computed the intercorrelations between the various balance-test scores. Out of twenty-one correlations, only three were significant. The range was −.17 to .53 and the average was .12. He found that certain of the balances measured improved during the course in swimming, but the correlation between improvement in swimming and improvement in balance was not significant.

---

[35] *Ibid.,* p. 219.

[36] John C. Bachman, "Specificity vs. Generality in Learning and Performing Two Large Muscle Motor Tasks," *Research Quarterly,* XXXII:1, Part 1 (March 1961), 3–11.

[37] Robert William Tyler, "Interrelationships among Dynamic and Static Balance Measures, and their Correlation with Certain Sport Skills" (unpublished Master's thesis, The Pennsylvania State University, 1960).

[38] Ann Valentine, "The Effect of Selected Physical Education Activities on the Balancing Ability of College Women" (unpublished Master's thesis, The Pennsylvania State University, 1961).

[39] John A. Reeves, "A Study of Various Types of Balance and Their Relationship to Swimming Endurance and Speed" (unpublished Master's thesis, The Pennsylvania State University, 1962).

DISCUSSION

That the low intercorrelations between balance tests indicate a high degree of specificity is clear. It is also clear that only certain types of balance tests have any significant correlation with even those skills in which balance seems to be an important factor. If we define balance as adjustment in body control with respect to the pull of gravity, we are faced with the fact that some type of balance is a part of every activity. We can hardly say that this adjustment is an "insignificant" part of sport skill. The above findings of low or no relationship between certain sport skills and selected balance measures seem to mean that we did not measure the balances involved; *i.e.,* balance is highly specific to each position, static or dynamic. Of course, the many other variables in a complex skill may greatly obscure any variation due to differences in the levels of the balances involved. Granting basic amounts of balance abilities to all subjects who can walk, run, and change direction, perhaps *additional amounts* are of minor importance, having little to do with the relative rank of these individuals as they progress to higher levels in certain activities. This hypothesis is applicable to other correlational studies reporting no significant "r's," and to certain hypotheses as to transfer. If the basic amounts are already present in all subjects previous to the training, additional amounts are of so little importance as to be indiscernible.

The view of McGeoch, Hebb, and others that new learning is built on past learning, and that adult learning is almost always affected by transfer, was presented in earlier chapters. Hebb expressed the opinion that the reason we do not find transfer in learning experiments is because the transfer effects have already taken place before the experiment starts.[40] This concept is closely related to the "basic abilities" hypothesis; *i.e.,* one learns ways to learn and one acquires abilities which are applicable in many similar situations. There seem to be many abilities which affect the earliest stages of learning in the beginner, and many of these are nonmotor. Those of the readers who have attempted to teach skills to groups with very low I.Q.s will be aware of the lack in many of these subjects of the ability to "get the general idea" of what to do.

It seems to me that we cannot entirely divorce previously developed bases, motor and nonmotor, from the learning of a new skill; and many of these bases do not seem to be "identical elements." However, the amount of specificity in the learning of the particular motor task is extremely high, as hundreds of low to zero correlations have shown. Failure to recognize this fact has led to much wasted time and many false predictions through use of "general motor ability" and "motor educability" tests. Henry's interpretation [41] of the differences in aptitudes (and the positive correlation of some

---

[40] D. O. Hebb, *The Organization of Behavior* (New York: Science Editions, Inc., 1961), p. 110.

[41] Henry, "Specificity vs. Generality in Learning Motor Skills," p. 127.

of these motor-ability batteries with achievement) as being due to variation in the number of specific abilities individuals possess seems to describe most learning beyond infancy and the earliest stages of the novice. It will certainly not lead us into as many *cul-de-sacs* as has the general-ability hypothesis.

One other point seems to be suggested by the review of the previous studies on specificity: the fallacy of trying to draw a line of demarcation between fine and gross motor skills. On the one hand, the so-called fine motor skills must be built over a postural base involving many larger muscles. The degree of involvement of the gross musculature seems to vary along a continuum, but never approaches zero. Fine precisions involve precise postural controls. On the other hand, higher levels of so-called gross motor skills involve small muscle action and many controls of a delicate nature.

LEARNING CURVES

In his study evaluating motor learning with heterogeneous groups, Henry says:

> Using the method of residuals to hold statistically constant the influence of initial skill, it is possible to compute derived learning scores which are unrelated to initial skill and at the same time substantially correlated with learning and also with post-learning performance.[42]

In Henry and Nelson's study, cited earlier, in which they examine the learning rates at different age levels, they say:

> Attempts to fit a mathematical curve system to these graphs in order to quantify the learning rates with greater accuracy have not been fully satisfactory due to the irregularity of the points.[43]

They conclude as follows:

> Evidently, the 10-year-old differs from the 15-year-old in being slower in motor performance of the type measured. On the average, he learns more than the older boy before the plateau is reached, but probably approaches the plateau at the same rate. His final skill is more determined by his ability to learn than is characteristic of the 15-year-old.[44]

Bachman [45] compared the learning curves of ten groups of male subjects and ten groups of female subjects during learning sessions on a stabilometer and on a free-standing ladder. He reported that rate of learning was not influenced by age or sex over the range of six to twenty-six years. Performance level (skill) varied considerably with age and was relatively poor

---

[42] Henry, "Evaluation of Motor Learning When Performance Levels Are Heterogeneous," p. 176 (in abstract), *Research Quarterly*, 27 (May 1956), 176.

[43] Henry and Nelson, *op. cit.*, p. 172.

[44] *Ibid.*, p. 175.

[45] Bachman, "Motor Learning and Performance as Related to Age and Sex in Two Measures of Balance Coordination," *Research Quarterly*, 32 (May 1961), 123–137.

in post-adolescent females. The average learning rate was considerably slower for the free-standing ladder climb than it was for the balance-board stabilometer. He noted a slowing of learning rate on the stabilometer during adolescence but a speeding up of the rate for the ladder climb during the same period.

PREDICTION

Welch [46] extended Bachman's study, having her subjects practice the free-standing ladder climb for six days (sixty trials), where Bachman had used ten trials. She reported a multiple "R" of .75 by the thirtieth practice, using initial score and improvement as her factors for predicting final level. In other words, the prediction was relatively poor half-way through the training period.

Trussell [47] had forty college women learn a three-ball juggling skill during twenty-seven practice periods spaced over nine weeks. She found no appreciable correlation between any of the cumulated learning scores and the initial score (range from −.19 to .09). Cumulated learning scores correlated progressively higher with final success score as the practice continued. She combined periods 1 and 2 for her initial score, then combined periods 3 and 4, 5 and 6, 8 through 11, 12 through 15, and 16 through 19. The complete learning score was the improvement from periods 1 and 2 to periods 24 through 27. The correlations of cumulated learning with final score were: .09, .32, .38, .52, .54, and .59 (cumulative starting with 3 and 4 and continuing up to and including 16 through 19, correlated with 24 through 27).

Trussell concludes in part as follows:

> . . . The learning curve of 3-ball juggling shows that this skill is acquired relatively slowly compared with other laboratory-type motor-learning tasks. While 50 per cent of the learning is achieved after 4 days of practice, 11 days of practice are needed to secure 75 per cent of the learning and approximately 21 days of practice are required to reach 90 per cent.
>
> The effectiveness of prediction of individual differences in final success, made on the basis of multiple correlations using initial skill and some specified amount of practice, rises almost linearly during the first 60 per cent of practice. Relatively little increase in predictability is achieved by including the last 40 per cent of practice even though nearly 20 per cent of the learning occurs during this interval.[48]

The above finding of slight improvement in predictability during the last 40 per cent of the learning might very well be accounted for by the variations in levels at which individuals reach their limit. If individuals were reaching plateaus at differing levels during this last 40 per cent of the

---

[46] Marya Welch, "Prediction of Motor Skill Attainment from Early Learning," *Perceptual and Motor Skills,* XVII (1963), 263–66.

[47] Ella Trussell, "Prediction of Success in a Motor Skill on the Basis of Early Learning Achievement," *Research Quarterly,* XXXVI:3 (October 1965), 342–47.

[48] *Ibid.,* pp. 346–47.

learning, the wide individual variation in improvement rates would account for the low increase in predictability from the later practice scores.

Hengst [49] completed a study using thirty-two female subjects in the learning of a dynamic balance skill. Her apparatus was a continuous seventy-two foot balance beam which decreased in width one-quarter inch every twelve feet. The beam was one-and-one-half inches wide for the first twelve feet, and one-quarter inch wide for the last twelve feet. Each subject practiced ten days, four trials each day, for a total of forty trials. She calculated a first order correlation between cumulative learning score at each session and the final score. Her Pearson product-moment "r" was .867 using cumulative scores at the sixth day, but only .876 between the ninth day and the final score of the tenth day.

Morehouse [50] used the raw data from Hengst's problem to determine if prediction of final success in this balancing skill could be improved by multiple correlation techniques. A multiple correlation of .764 with final performance (tenth day) was found by using a combination of initial performance and cumulative learning over the first three days of practice. These results seem to be consistent with the correlations obtained by Trussell in the three-ball juggling skill.

I.Q. AND MOTOR LEARNING

The literature on the relationship of academic intelligence test scores to motor learning scores is so extensive and so uniform in its findings that mere mention will be made of it. In general, correlations range from zero to .50, with the average being .20 or less. When motor learning is correlated with intelligence in groups of lower intelligence levels, a somewhat higher relationship tends to appear. From the moron level down in the scale, the correlation tends to become higher; *i.e.*, the moron tends to be superior to the imbecile in learning motor skills. In selected samples of those well above I.Q. 100, such as senior high school or college students, the correlations tend to approach zero.

prediction of athletic success [51]

The same conclusions as those reported by industrial psychologists in their field have been reached from studies of prediction of athletic success at the high levels; namely, the best predictive test of ability is a sampling of performance in the activity in which prediction is desired. However, as pointed out above with regard to studies of learning, initial score has little or no relationship to amount or rate of improvement. One can use such

---

[49] Virginia G. Hengst, "Predictive Ability of the Modified Springfield Beam Walking Test and a Seventy-Two Foot Balance Beam Walking Test" (unpublished Master of Education problem, The Pennsylvania State University, 1965).

[50] C. A. Morehouse, "Addendum" to Hengst, *op. cit.*

[51] John D. Lawther, *Psychology of Coaching* (Englewood Cliffs, N.J.: Prentice-Hall, Inc., 1951), pp. 67–70.

batteries of tests to sort out the opposite tails of the curve, if doing so is necessary and desirable. However, observation at one practice would probably be at least as effective unless the numbers of subjects was quite large. The discriminations between individuals near the mean are much more difficult to make, and the test prediction is always a certain score plus or minus the standard error. For example, a correlation of .80 between the criterion and the test used for prediction means that the distribution can be limited to 60 per cent of its original size; *i.e.,* instead of picking by pure chance from the entire distribution, we can now pick the individuals from a distribution only 60 per cent as large ($k = \sqrt{1 - r^2}$). However, individual selection of the most skillful presents additional problems. Morehouse summarizes these as follows: [52]

1. Ability to predict at extremes is dependent on the spread of the scores in the skill test. The more widely spread the scores are, the better are the chances of prediction.
2. Individuals vary in performance from day to day and even from hour to hour.
3. The criterion with which the test is correlated is not a true criterion in itself because of errors in judgment of even the most expert raters.
4. The basic assumption of prediction is that the distributions of both skill-test scores and criteria are normal. This assumption could scarcely be made of the subjects in the typical athletic squad which reports for practice.

Computed probabilities of selecting from one to five of the best players from a squad of twenty-five by use of scores in a test correlating .80 with a completely valid and reliable criterion, follow. These estimates are based on a normal distribution in which the estimate of the variance is an adjustment of individual predictions, using rank scores.[53]

Estimate of the probability of getting all five correct or one chance out of 100	.0102
Estimate of the probability of being wrong on all five	.0776
Estimate of the probability of being correct on four and wrong on one	.0767
Estimate of the probability of being correct on one and wrong on four	.2592
Estimate of the probability of being correct on three and wrong on two	.2334
Estimate of the probability of being correct on two and wrong on three	.3461

Prediction of future national or world records in various individual sports events has been attempted many times, along an exponential decline.

---

[52] If $r = .00$, $\sigma = 7.36$; if $r = .80$, $\sigma = 4.416$. The computations and statements were prepared and summarized by C. H. Morehouse.

[53] See Robert G. Steel and James H. Torrie, *Principles and Procedures of Statistics* (New York: McGraw-Hill Book Company, 1960). Consult page 175 under "A Prediction and Its Variance."

Henry's [54] short article and graph of the records in the mile run over a century is quite interesting in the light of such attempts. He presents the graph and says:

> Recent events can best be appreciated by examining the lower right corner of the graph in relation to earlier data. The lesson is clear. Neither consistency of performance nor trend of the empirical improvement curve gives us any dependable information about the physiological limits of human performance.[55]

There are numerous examples of misinterpretation of athletic prediction tests in the literature. A study by Boyd *et al.*,[56] abstracted in the October 1955 issue of *Research Quarterly,* has been quoted in a recent Tests and Measurement text as evidence that the Knox Test of Basketball Ability is an excellent instrument for prediction of basketball success. The one figure which is quoted is the biserial "r" of .96 between the test scores and membership or nonmembership on the basketball squad (after the coach cut his squad to less than half its original size). The investigators deserve a more thorough report because they present much more valuable evidence in their study than the biserial correlation involving forty-two men and what may not have been a normal distribution.

The additional data, besides the statistics on retention (eighteen men) and dropping (twenty-four men) from the squad, included:

1. Knox Test scores.
2. Coach ranking of all squad members after three weeks of practice.
3. Coach ranking of retained players at end of season.
4. $\dfrac{\text{Total minutes played}}{\text{Number of games played}}$, or average playing time per game.
5. $\dfrac{\text{Points scores}}{\text{Total minutes of game participation}}$, or average points per minutes of play.

The respective correlations were (rho was used for those involving rank):

$r_{12} = .17$ An examination of the correlation of the Knox Test scores with
$r_{13} = .10$ all the other criteria (r_{12}, r_{13}, r_{14}, r_{15}) indicates no value. As to
$r_{14} = .00$ the coach's original gross selection and its high biserial correlation
$r_{15} = .11$ with the Knox Test, the coach would probably prefer to make the
$r_{23} = .27$ judgment because he has additional data as to player personal
$r_{24} = .23$ characteristics, academic aptitude, and attitudes toward improve-
$r_{25} = .52$ ment, training, work, and winning. The inexperienced coach or
$r_{34} = .85$ teacher might wish to use a test to make the release from the
$r_{35} = .79$ squad seem to the student to be more impersonal and objective.
$r_{45} = .11$

[54] Franklin M. Henry, "A Note on Physiological Limits and the History of the Mile Run," *Research Quarterly,* XXV:4 (December 1954), 483–84.

[55] *Ibid.,* p. 484.

[56] C. A. Boyd, J. R. McCachren, and I. F. Waglow, "Predictive Ability of a Selected Basketball Test," *Research Quarterly,* XXIII:3 (October 1955), 364–65.

sport skill tests

Studies have been published describing construction and validation of numerous sport-skill tests for badminton, basketball, baseball, softball, field hockey, touch football, golf, gymnastics and tumbling, handball, soccer, diving and swimming, tennis, volleyball, and other sports.

One common procedure in constructing such tests is to correlate individual scores on various skills selected from the sport with experts' rating of those same individuals in that sport. The assumption is that a high correlation of skill scores with judges' ratings establishes the validity of the test. Items which do not correlate significantly with expert ratings are deleted from the battery.

Other procedures are: to correlate the skill scores and total battery score with the subjects' ranks in a round-robin tournament; to correlate skill test battery scores of teams with team success in games (wins) within the group tested; and to correlate scores on a newly constructed test with other tests already available. Reliability is computed by the test-retest method. One problem in the determination of reliability by the test-retest method in sports is the fact that players fluctuate considerably from performance to performance; hence a reliability coefficient close to 1.00 would not only be very difficult to obtain but would not actually be a true measure; *i.e.*, it would have to be so crude in discrimination as to gloss over the individual fluctuations.

A check of reported validities of twenty-five different sport-skill tests reported in the literature revealed five which reported a validity coefficient of .85 or higher, seven in the .80 to .84 range, two in the .75 to .79 range, one in the .70 to .74 range, four in the .65 to .69 range, four in the .60 to .64 range, and one reporting a validity coefficient of only .44. Most of these validities are too low to be of much value for individual prediction. These tests can perhaps be used at times with advantage for teaching purposes, motivating purposes, or for gross classification with large numbers, although even in gross classification only the extremes of the curve are valuable. The discrimination is not fine enough to classify the middle 68 per cent.

It is unfortunate that we are not able to measure objectively and then predict accurately in the sports field but, so far, we have not found objective tests in team and dual sports which can replace the subjective judgment of the expert. Fortunately, individual sports—track, archery, rifle, bowling—can be objectively measured by chronometers and measures of distance or of accuracy. Three major problems seem to account for the difficulty in constructing skill tests with high enough validity to serve for individual selection or for prediction of later success. The problem of predicting rate and amount of improvement has already been discussed in the first part of this chapter. Initial scores, even if they are well above average, have too low a relationship with improvement scores and final scores for use in prediction.

A second problem is the impossibility of measuring many of the factors which contribute to success in highly complex sports; *e.g.*, personality factors, attitudes, adjustments to stress. A third problem is that the specific items used, even if they are parts taken out of the activity itself, do not represent the same performance when isolated as they do when integrated into the larger patterns of whole activity performance.

This last problem, mentioned by Morehouse under "Prediction of Athletic Success," is also applicable to these sport-skill tests when "expert judgment" is used as a criterion. The writer is reminded of a conclusion which appeared at the end of a study in the *Research Quarterly* some fifteen years ago:

> There is no relation between improvement in swimming form and improvement in swimming speed for either the crawl stroke or the breast stroke. The coefficients of correlation between improvement in form and improvement in speed ranged from −0.11 to 0.11.[57]

The above statement startled the writer because form (implying efficient form) is a way of doing, a work method; and what better criterion do we have for efficient form than actual achievement in performance! Here one can clearly see how variations in viewpoint enter into one common criterion for skill-test validity, the "judgment of experts." In precisely measurable, individual events involving distance, speed, or accuracy (marksmanship, track and field, bowling), and perhaps round-robin or ladder tournaments in individual sports, we do not have to rely so much on expert judgment. But in spite of its subjectivity and occasional error, we have not yet been able to find any means of evaluation of dual or team-sport ability which even approaches the validity of expert judgment. However, there are certain basic conditions; namely,

1. the one so judging must be really expert, not just some dubious "authority";
2. the expert must have first made careful observations of the individuals to be judged over an adequate span of time; and he must have been able to make comparisons of the respective individuals during performance;
3. the expert must have made (at least mentally) a rough outline of a case history of each individual to be judged, in the various behavior situations and performances, competitive and otherwise.

SUMMARY

Learning is measured in terms of rate, amount and difficulty of improvement. Rates and amounts of learning by individuals cannot be compared unless the levels at which they are working are the same; hence the measurement must be adjusted to take into account the difficulty of improving as one advances to the higher levels. If we wish to compare rates of learning of individuals who are at different levels of skill, we must interpret the scores so that they represent results of equivalent lengths and conditions of practice.

Perhaps an average rate per skill, established by large groups at each level, would be the best standard for comparison and analysis of the indi-

---

[57] Dillon, *op. cit.*, p. 8.

vidual learner. Insofar as learning is specific to the skill, we would have to establish such learning curves for each skill; *i.e.,* we could not predict from one skill the learning rate in another.

Individual performance at any one time varies with background of experience and training, fatigue, interest and motivation, and physiological variations. Initial scores are of little or no predictive value as to rate of learning and final achievement level.

Neither per cent gain of initial scores nor amount of change in raw scores is a valid measure of improvement. With practice time held constant, cumulative learning scores and per cent gain of "amount left before limit is reached" seem to produce reasonably valid and comparable measures of improvement.

So-called "motor educability" and "general motor-ability" tests do not measure individual aptitude for learning or predict an individual's approximate degree of final attainment. General motor-ability tests are invalid because motor abilities are specific to the learning task. An individual has specific aptitudes, not general motor ability. These aptitudes are specific to the skill being learned; *i.e.,* individual rate of learning varies from task to task. Those individuals who seem to be "very good" in physical activities merely have a lot of special aptitudes; those who seem "poor" have very few.

Great breadth and great quantity of background experience in motor learning does seem to build bases which accelerate the learning of similar types of motor skills, at least in the earlier stages. The farther along one progresses in the complex physical skills, the more specific they seem to become; *i.e.,* training in one skill does not seem to improve one's performance in another skill unless there is great similarity in the motor acts.

As mentioned previously, the final level of attainment in a motor skill cannot be predicted from an initial score. Combinations of initial scores with cumulative learning scores (in a multiple "R") begins to have some predictive value about half-way through the learning, in simpler skills. Academic intelligence does not seem to be a factor related to the learning of motor skills except at the lower end of the I.Q. range.

So far, tests have not been devised which are of much value in predicting individual success in athletics. Subjective as it is, the expert teacher's or coach's judgment is still far superior to test batteries for individual selection. The numerous sport-skill tests in the field of physical education may be of value as teaching devices, for motivation purposes, or for a crude classification of the extremes (not the group ± 1 sigma) when very large numbers make individual observation impractical. Such tests are not an adequate measure to use for the evidence of either the learning or the final achievement in the instructional program; *i.e.,* course grade. As to predictive value for future learning, the principle is the same as was reported under prediction of learning: initial score has no correlation or a negative correlation with improvement.

discussion questions

1. Is initial performance in a motor skill a good indication of the final skill level which the individual will attain?
2. Is rate of improvement negatively correlated with initial score?
3. Is learning best measured in terms of per cent of the initial score represented by each practice gain?
4. Should the same quantity in a raw improvement score have different values at higher and lower levels of learning?
5. Do "motor educability" tests measure aptness for learning?
6. Is there such a thing as "general motor ability"?
7. Does one's aptness for motor learning vary with the skill being practiced?
8. Is the Stanford Motor Skills Unit an excellent predictor of level of success in industrial manual-motor skills?
9. Does specificity of learning rule out the possibility of transferable basic abilities?
10. Do group learning curves vary from skill to skill?
11. Can final attainment be precisely predicted half-way through the training period?
12. Should athletic- or sport-skill tests be used by the coach or teacher as the criterion for squad and team selection?
13. Should the teacher use objective sport-skill tests as his measures of skill-course outcomes and as a basis for student grade in the course?
14. Is academic intelligence of a high order essential for high achievement in motor-skill learning?

Subject Index

Attention:
  diffused, 56–57
  direction of, 58, 59, 60
  focus of, 51, 55, 57

Balance, 134–135
Binet Simon Test, Stanford Revision, 20

Changes, not learning: growth, fluctuation, senescence, 3, 4
Child development, hypothetical concepts, 16–21
  retarded, 16–21
Computer analogy (*see* Learning)
Concept, 47
Constant error, 60, 76–77
Creative imagination, 41

Distraction, 75–76

Emotion:
  athletes' reactions to, 119–120
  changes with intensity, 106–107, 112
  chemical and physiological changes, 109–110
  definition, 105, 109
  a subjective feeling, 107–108
  weaknesses in experimental studies, 110
Errors (*see* Methods)

Feedback:
  loop-control, automatic (*see* Readjustments during response)

Generalizations, 47–48, 68

High-skill level, 79–80

Imitation, 50–52
Incentives, 104–105
Individual differences, 68, 69, 77
Institute of Achievement of Human Potentials, 16

Juggling, 58–59

Kinesthesis, 57
Knowledge of mechanical principles, 99–101
Knowledge of results, 98–99
Kraus-Weber Scores, 20

Learning:
  adult, differences in, 67
  amount of, methods of computation, 124–127
  analogy to computer, 2–3
  animal vs. human, 12
  automatic action, 43–44
  beginner characteristics, 65
  cause, 2
  change with age, 22
  change with experience, 5–6, 28
  complexity, 34–36, 46
  conditioning, 37–38
  connectionism (bond formation), 38–39
  a continuum, 34, 39
  definition, 2, 4
  drive or purpose, 35
  gestalt, 39–40, 42
  hemispheric dominance, 17, 18–19
  hierarchies, 4–5, 13
  individuation, 7–8, 11
  individuation of body-part, 9–10
  latent, 36
  laterality, 17, 18–19
  levels of consciousness, 50–52, 55
  vs. maturation, 6–7

Author Index